Traditional Derbyshire Fare

300 recipes
plus the stories and anecdotes
behind them

Jill Armitage

Published by Sigma Leisure – an imprint of
Sigma Press, Stobart House, Pontyclerc, Penybanc Road
Ammanford, Carmarthenshire SA18 3HP
www.sigmapress.co.uk

British Library Cataloguing in Publication Data

A CIP record for this book is available from the British Library

ISBN: 978-1-85058-872-6

Typesetting and Design by: Sigma Press, Ammanford, Carmarthenshire

Photographs: Jill Armitage

Cover photograph: Bakewell Old House Museum

Printed by: Akcent Media Limited

Dedicated with all my love to Dena and Sophia

Contents

Introduction

Even before Arbor Low, the Stonehenge of Derbyshire was built a few hundred thousand years ago, Derbyshire was a county rich in tasty natural resources – gastronomically speaking. In the forests lived deer and wild boar. The land yielded wild strawberries, blackberries, sour crab apples, small hard pears, cobnuts and fungi. The Romans introduced rabbit, hare and pheasant. The Anglo-Saxons cultivated cider-apple trees and kept bees for honey. They brought from their continental homelands the arts of brewing and baking, and the techniques for making butter and cheese. They made ale from the barley and worked the ground grains with water to form a dough that cooked on flat stones before open fires. By the 11th century, the Anglo-Saxons had established the basis of our national cuisine – solid, yeoman like fare designed to sustain a man. This was the food that was destined to feed Derbyshire folks for the next thousand plus years – meat, bread, cheese and ale. Nourishing, economical, readily available and simple, it was only natural that this should become our staple diet.

But things were about to change. In 1066 William the Norman Conqueror landed in England and apart from moving in and taking over, the Normans with their curious ideas, revolutionized the Saxon way of life in the kitchen. They prepared such delicacies as tripe and onions, and made dishes with wonderful pastry. They had salt and pepper on the table and flavoured their dishes not only with herbs but with strange tasting spices that the Saxons later knew as ginger, cloves, nutmeg and cinnamon. The Norman cooks were inventive and the simple cooking of England became embellished with glamour. It is to this time that we can trace many regional dishes that have been kept alive by country cooks working in their own kitchens and passing down this culinary know-how from one generation to the next. But locating these dishes needed research and inspiration from many sources, the main one being my grandmother's cookery book with its weird and wonderful collection of recipes which date back over a hundred years. This started me on a cookery book trail and the discovery of many far older books in the local authorities collection.

In Derby library I found the household book of Peter Geary who was Bailiff of Derby in 1610 and 1619 – prior to the introduction of Mayors in 1638. Peter Geary's House Hand Book gives interesting recipes for cooking large quantities like Derby Cake which begins *'take a strike of flour, 8lbs of sugar'*.

Jane Mosley's hand written recipes from 1690 are an inspiration and I've included several here to show just how similar they are to those we are familiar with today. Jane Mosley was a literate, well-to-do woman of her day, born in August 1669 to a wealthy family who originated from a 16th century Ashbourne mercer. Jane Mosley's book of recipes and cures was probably written as part of her preparation for marriage and housekeeping when in 1697, she married Edward Soresby, a grazier and arable farmer with 117 acres of land at Darley, near Matlock.

Their standard of living was high, her recipes were mainly for entertaining with lavish use of wine for cooking, imported oranges, lemons, dried fruits and spices. Jane Mosley gives us an idea of what kind of foods were being eaten by the well to do during the reign of William and Mary. She tells us how to bake such 17th and 18th century delicacies as calves chalderon, eels, oyster pye, chewet of stockfish, neates tongue, larks, sparrows, blackbirds, swan, wild goose, mallard, curlew, hearneshaw and woodcocks. When we read such suggestions as *'let the heads hang out for show'*, and ingredients like *'a peele of lead'*, which we now realise is probably the quickest way to poison your nearest and dearest, it goes without saying that the majority of these recipes would not delight our modern taste buds.

At Derbyshire Record office, amongst others is Mary Swanick's handwritten recipe book from 1743 which contains more than 100 recipes. This gives an interesting look at such delicacies as stewed whole calf's head, crud loaves, and squichanary pye.

Alison Uttley, the Derbyshire writer produced over a hundred books and is best known for her *Little Grey Rabbit* books. Born Alice Jane Taylor on December 17th 1884, as a child she lived at a lonely farm between Lea and Cromford, and wrote about her Derbyshire childhood in her book *Recipes From An Old Farmhouse*. There's more recollecting than recipes, but it's a rare insight into a bygone age when cookery was an important part of domestic life.

During the mid to latter half of last century, my mother was an active member of the Women's Institute so I checked out the first recipe book of the Derbyshire Federation of Women's Institutes printed in 1953. This is a compilation of valued family recipes collected from members, with titles like House Cake, Mother's Parkin, Derbyshire Oatcakes, Wakes Cake, Cuddlastone Cake and of course the jams that the WI is identified with.

While a member of Chatsworth Ladies Circle my own family's culinary contributions went into a book which we sold in aid of the Portland Training College Appeal. But this was the 70s/80s and the tendency was to abandon these time-honoured recipes in favour of the cuisine of the countries visited on holiday, a trend that has continued. Over the past fifty years, we have been all too eager to step out of those past centuries and embrace a more cosmopolitan lifestyle along with adopting dishes that have no relation-ship what-so-ever with our past.

Apart from the invasion of different cultures, British tastes have also been changed by a subtler, yet no less persuasive invasion; canned and frozen food, packaged meals, mass produced poultry and factory-made bread. We are no longer an agricultural county. Less than one worker in 100 toils on the land, yet we enjoy the far reaching produce of a global market which has radically altered our tastes and eating habits.

For this reason, if they are not preserved, recipes that have been handed down intact from generation to generation in many country kitchens around Derbyshire are about to disappear. The more countrified the region, the more such recipes have survived which is why Derbyshire's rural fare has remained stubbornly and proudly independent.

Most of the recipes in this book are survivors from the past. They deserve to survive because they show the creativity of countless generations that have not only kept them alive, but have also added their own distinct dash of originality and flavour. A few of these Derbyshire dishes, like the Bakewell Pudding, have gained national popularity; many more, including some of the most delectable, are still little known outside the places whose name they bear. Give them a try! This isn't just food, this is food that is rooted in expediency and marked by its ancestral heritage. Its individual, easy, economical, readily available, and has a strong regional accent. This isn't just food, this is Derbyshire food at its very best.

Conversion Rates

Grandmothers style of cooking meant throwing everything in without weighing, based on a dash of wisdom, a cup of experience and a spoonful of luck. Recipes were used for guidance and the old recipes in this book were originally in imperial measures, so here is a convenient conversion table from imperial to metric.

Capacity

imperial	metric
¼ pint	150 ml
½ pint	275 ml
¾ pint	425 ml
1 pint	570 ml
1½ pints	850 ml
2 pints	1.2 litre
3 pints	1.7 litre
4 pints	2.25 litre
5 pints	2.9 litre

½ pint is roughly equal to 1 American measuring cup, breakfast cup, mug or 2 gills

¼ pint is roughly equal to 1 English tea cup or 1 gill

7 tablespoons (serving spoons) water are roughly equal to ¼ pint

Mass

imperial	metric
½oz	10g
1oz	25g
2oz	50g
3oz	75g
4oz	110g
5oz	150g
6oz	175g
8oz	225g
10oz	275g
12oz	350g
16oz	450g
1lb	450g
2lb	900g
3lb	1.35kg
4lb	1.80kg
5lb	2.25kg

oz — ounce   lb — pound
g — gram(s)   kg — kilogram

The use of spoons and cups is a bit more haphazard:

The smallest spoon is the salt spoon which is equal to ten good pinches of salt

2 salt spoons = 1 egg spoon
3 salt spoons = 1 teaspoon

1 level teaspoon = $\frac{1}{6}$ oz (5g) salt or flour but $\frac{1}{3}$ oz (10g) sugar, syrup, jam, jelly or treacle

2 teaspoons = 1 dessertspoon
4 teaspoons = 1 tablespoon

1 dessertspoon sugar, syrup, jam, jelly or treacle = ½ oz (10g)

2 dessertspoons = 1 tablespoon

1 tablespoon sugar, syrup, jam, jelly or treacle = 1oz (25g)

1 tablespoon flour = ½oz (10g) but 1 heaped tablespoon of flour = 1oz (25g)

1 breakfast cup flour = 4-5oz (110-150g)

1 breakfast cup sugar = 8oz (225g)

1 teacup breadcrumbs = 2oz (50g)

right and middle right: When preparing vegetables never discard the rough bits, the tough bits, the stalk and the outside leaves
far right: Make a pottage out of vegetables boiled in stock

Soups and Pottage

The essential utensil of the medieval kitchen was a cast-iron pot or cauldron in which all manner of 'pottage' could be created. In fact, pottage comes from old French *potage* meaning contents of a pot. With a chain and hook, pots and skillets could be raised or lowered over the fire, and most pots had tripod feet so they could also stand firmly among the embers.

Pottage was a soup-like stew and for many centuries was part of the staple diet. At its most basic it consisted of vegetables boiled in stock. When preparing vegetables, the rough bits, the tough bits, stalks and outside leaves were never discarded. They were all chopped or shredded, and put in the pot with enough boiling water to cover. As cooking methods changed, this was either put in the bottom of the oven for a few hours, or left to simmer on the hob. When the vegetables were soft, they would be pounded to a pulp, seasoned with salt and pepper and the resultant pottage served hot with chunks of bread.

Nearly everything that was edible would end up in the pot. If a visitor joined in the meal, he would be invited to dip in, taking a chance on scooping up some choice morsels. From this we get the word 'pot-luck' – a term to express the idea of random choice.

Pottage now tends to be the name given to a thick meat or vegetable soup. Another name is broth, a liquid which contains the juices and flavourings of meat and bones with diced vegetables and cereal added. The poor relation made from boiling oatmeal in water with possibly a splash of milk is called gruel.

Derbyshire Broth

The basis of a good, nourishing soup or broth is the stock which is usually obtained by boiling a ham bone, a marrow bone, a chicken or game carcase.

Place the bones and any diced meat in a pan. Cover with 2 pints of water and bring to the boil. Add 2 tablespoons rice or barley, cover and simmer for 1 hour. Dice 1 stalk celery, ½ medium turnip, 1 carrot, and 1 onion. Add to the pan with a good pinch of salt and pepper and simmer for a further 30 minutes. Remove fat and bones before serving.

White Soup

Peel and slice 4 large potatoes and put in a pan. Sprinkle with salt and cover with 2 pints (1.2 litre) of water. Bring to the boil, reduce heat and add 2 sliced onions, a slice of white bread, 6 pepper corns and a blade of mace. Simmer until tender then rub through a sieve and return to the clean pan with 1 pint milk and 2 tablespoons sago. Sago is a starchy cereal used for puddings and as a thickening agent. Bring to the boil then simmer again for 10 minutes, stirring frequently.

Thrifty Brown Soup

Take previously cooked bones from a roast, cover with water, bring to the boil then allow to simmer until the bones show small holes. Remove the bones. Put the liquid aside to cool and remove the fat. To the liquid add any water in which vegetables have been boiled, ½ chopped onion and 1 chopped celery stalk. Colour with a little gravy browning and thicken with flour or oatmeal.

far left: Stock is usually obtained by boiling bones
left: A tasty bowl of soup

Mayfield Onion Soup

Peel and chop ½lb (225g) shallots and ½lb (225g) onions. Heat 2oz (56.7g) butter in a pan, add the onions and fry to a pale gold. Add 1 tablespoon flour, a twist of salt and pepper, then 1 pint of stock. Simmer for three minutes, add 1 teaspoon mustard and serve. Apparently, if you peel onions upside down, this reduces the output of the pungent chemicals that make you cry.

A bowl of Mayfield Onion Soup, thick with onions and shallots

Mushroom Soup

Many parks and woodlands are prime habitats for wild mushroom hunting, but don't take any chances when collecting fungi. A comprehensive field guide is invaluable. You should never risk eating a mushroom unless you are completely confident of its identification, or buy from a recognised supplier.

Peel and slice 1 large onion and 6oz (175g) mushrooms. Heat 1oz (25g) butter in a pan and toss in the chopped onion. When beginning to go transparent, add the mushrooms and season with a twist of salt and pepper. Turn the heat low and allow to cook for a minute before sprinkling on 1 tablespoon flour and adding ¾ pint (425ml) stock. Simmer for three minutes. Add ¾ pint (425ml) milk, remove from the heat and liquidise before serving.

Lettuce Soup

Wash 3 or 4 lettuces and put in a pan with 2oz (50g)) margarine, I chopped onion and 2-3 diced carrots. Simmer for 20 minutes. Mix 1½oz (35g) cornflour to a smooth paste with a little milk. Add this and 2 pints (1.2 litre) of milk to the lettuces and simmer for ¾ hour. Rub through a sieve and return to the saucepan with a teaspoon chopped parsley, season to taste, reheat and just before serving, add the yolk of an egg.

Mock Hare Soup

Make a stock from lentils or brown haricots, 1 carrot, 1 turnip, 1 onion, 1 stick celery all cut small. Add ½ teaspoon mixed herbs, 1 tablespoon gravy essence, ½ tin tomatoes, 1 bay leaf, few sprigs of parsley. Allow to simmer gently for two hours, then pass through a sieve. Melt 2oz (50g) butter in pan, stir in 1oz (25g) flour allow to cook until turning golden then add stock, reheat and serve.

Poacher's Soup

Although this is definitely more meaty than the previous dishes, by definition this is an improvised dish made from whatever furred or feathered game comes to hand.

Put a game carcass into a pan with 1 onion, 1 carrot, 1 teaspoon sugar and a bunch of herbs or bouquet garni. Cover with water and allow to simmer for 2-3 hours. Strain. Add salt and pepper to season, the whites of 2 eggs, and 2oz (50g) minced liver. To thicken, blend 1 teaspoon arrowroot in a little water and add to the soup just before serving.

Serving a perfect soup

Allow the liquid to simmer gently, not boil continuously, as this will make the soup cloudy.

The addition of herbs gives any soup a better flavour, but herbs need to be extracted from the pan before thickening or serving. To do this, tie the stalks together to make a bunch and loop the string round the handle of the pan for easy retrieval. Small or dried herbs like bay leaves, pepper corns and cloves, should be enclosed in a circle of fine cotton or muslin, gathered and tied to make a bag or bouquet garni. The traditional bouquet garni is made up of a bay leaf, sprig of parsley, and either thyme, sage, marjoram or rosemary. To thicken a soup, use rice, barley, sago, oatmeal, arrowroot, cornflour or flour.

Always test your soup before serving to check the flavour. Add salt and pepper to taste. If a soup is too salty, lower a lump of sugar on a spoon into the pot for a moment, or add a few slices of raw potato. This will absorb the salt and can be removed before serving.

Soups can be served with a sprinkle of chopped chives or parsley on top, a swirl of cream or a tablespoon of croutons.

A steaming bowl of soup with croutons

To make croutons

Take a slice of day old bread, cut into small cubes and deep fry. Drain well and scatter on the top of soup just before serving. Croutons are also used to sprinkle on or mix into salads.

Vegetables

In the mid 17th century, even the poor refused to eat vegetables. Root vegetables like turnips and swedes were considered to be dirty as they came from the ground and were regarded as cattle food. It took the likes of John Evelyn to produce vegetable recipes that made people no longer suspicious. Amongst other things, he was a leading figure in promoting good all round nutrition and a typical main course became known as 'meat and two veg'.

Sadly cooked vegetables were often limp and lifeless through over cooking. There was more goodness in the water they were boiled in than in the vegetables, but the water was generally used to make soup or gravy, so not all the nutrients were lost.

To minimalise vitamin loss, don't use too much water. Green leafy vegetables like spinach are best cooked by allowing the leaves to simply wilt over a low heat in their own liquid, the washing water left on the leaves, and ½ cup of salted water. Use a large pan and spread them rather than piling them high in a small pan. Bring them to the boil, turn down the heat, cover and simmer only until tender. Serve tossed in a little butter, a pinch of nutmeg and a twist of pepper.

When cooking vegetables like broccoli and cauliflower, put the thick end of the stalk in the boiling water and let the florets cook in the steam.

A slice of lemon, a tablespoon of sugar or bay leaf in water will reduce the odour of boiling cabbage and brussel sprouts.

A cup of milk or a squeeze of lemon juice added to the water when cooking cauliflower helps keep it white.

The loss of sweetness in vegetables is due to the time lapse after harvesting, so a spoonful of sugar

When cooking vegetables like broccoli and cauliflower, put the thick end of the stalk in the boiling water and let the florets cook in the steam

added to a pan of peas and carrots makes them taste sweeter. Sugar begins to revert to starch as soon as the plant is cut, so try to buy or grow fresh produce, then to enhance the flavour of peas even further, add a handful of pea pods to the cooking water.

Grow your own

Growing vegetables is now more of a hobby, but when money was scarce, people were unemployed or the pits were on short time it was a necessity that helped to feed the family. If people didn't have a garden they would have an allotment. If the weather was fit, early broad beans were planted in January and February. Shallots and onions, turnips and swedes went in during March. About Easter the men would be busy planting early potatoes and late broad beans. Gardeners considered it lucky to plant parsley, potatoes, beans and peas on Good Friday. April meant early peas and salad crops, and white cabbage seeds for Whitsun planting out. Towards the middle of April, carrots, beetroots and parsnips were set followed by peas. The bean row was then put up ready for May 12th, when except for a few late additions, the garden would be set. The paths would be edged with raspberry canes and other soft fruit, with flowers taking a minor role. Late summer meant flower and vegetable shows where the amateur gardeners showed their produce.

Wild and free

When considering vegetables, the wild leafy greens such as dandelions, chickweed, hogweed, fat hen, nettles, wild garlic and watercress can't be ignored. Of all the wild greens the nettle is one of the most prolific, and one of the easiest wild plants to recognise, if only because of its sting.

As a vegetable, nettles are very rich in vitamin C, iron, natural histamines, formic and silicic acid. Served as a vegetable or a drink, (see Nettle Tea and Nettle Beer) nettles are believed to have the ability to purify the blood, alleviate the discomfort of rheumatism, arthritis and pleurisy.

As a vegetable, nettles are rich in vitamin C, iron, natural histamines, formic and silicic acid

To prepare nettles

Young nettles have tender stalks which can be snipped off just above the ground and used whole. As the plant matures, use only the top leaves which are sweeter, but avoid nettles when the flower heads begin to form as they are course and not good for eating.

After a quick wash, pop the nettles into a pan with about a cup of boiling water and allow to simmer gently until tender. Drain and serve like spinach, but don't discard the cooking water (see nettle tea).

To make creamy nettles, cook as above then add a small knob of

butter and either a couple of tablespoons of cream or yogurt and season to taste. Cook gently for a further few minutes, stirring to coat then just before serving add a handful of either freshly chopped mint or parsley.

Dandelions

The common dandelion is one of the most versatile plants around. The flowers are used to make wine, and the roots can be dried and ground to make a substitute drink similar to coffee. The fresh leaves can be used as an addition to a salad or to make tea. Young dandelion roots make a delicious vegetable that can be peeled and cooked like carrots, and the leaves can be simmered gently like spinach. Pick the leaves when young, as age makes them bitter. If you boil the leaves, then strain off the liquid and discard before adding fresh water and bringing back to the boil, this should remove any bitterness. Serve with a knob of butter or as an alternative, cook with sliced onion, garlic and spices. Just before serving add a dash of lemon juice.

Melde - Fat Hen

One of Europe's oldest vegetables. Melde grows in the south of Derbyshire away from the limestone and gives its name to Melbourne or *Melde-Bourne* as the Saxons called it, meaning a stream where the melde grew abundantly. It is also known as 'Fat Hen'.

Take a stout plant, strip off the leaves and wash them thoroughly. Drain off all the liquid then wet again and place in a pan with just a little water and a pinch of salt. Boil for 10-15 minutes. Drain, press well and serve like spinach.

A field of golden dandelions as far as the eye can see

Potatoes

There's an old Derbyshire chant –

*Dearly beloved brethren, isn't it a sin
To eat roast* potatoes and throw
    away the skin
The skin feeds pigs and the pigs feed
    you
Dearly beloved brethren – don't you
    think its true*

* previous generations referred to baked potatoes as roast potatoes

We might not now feed potato peel to the pigs, but the chant still holds true – it is a sin to throw away the skin, particularly as in most cases the nutrients are stored just below this outer layer. The first stage in preparing potatoes should be to wash them. New potatoes can then be boiled and served in their skins to conserve nutrients. Older potatoes that contain more starch are better for mashing, frying or roasting, so after washing, peel the potatoes quite clumsily and put the chunky peel in a roasting dish. Sprinkle over a dribble of oil, salt and pepper and put into a moderate oven. After half an hour, shake them all up to ensure all the skin is crispy on the outside, return to the oven for ten minutes, then serve like crisps or savoury dips.

Lid Potatoes

And what better supper dish than a Lid Potato.

Bake large potatoes in their jackets in the oven for approximately an hour. If you insert a skewer through the centre of the potato before putting in the oven, heat is conducted through the skewer to the inside of the potato, which lessens the cooking time.

When the skins of the potatoes are brown and crisp, remove from the oven and neatly cut off the tops. Scoop all the potato out of the skins. Mash it up with a little salt and pepper and a lot of butter. Alternatively, combine the potato with mayonnaise, any diced, cooked meat, chopped chives, or grated cheese.

Push this back into the skins and place the tops back in place like little lids. Eat with a teaspoon.

Potato Bake

Finely slice a couple of potatoes and place in a shallow, ovenproof dish. For extra taste, add an onion too. Pour over ½ cup of milk and ½ cup cream. Dot with butter, sprinkle over salt, freshly ground pepper and a little nutmeg. Bake until the top is brown and the potatoes soft.

Jane Mosley's hand written recipe from 1690 refers to sallets (salad) which was cooked with butter and vinegar

SALLETS (translation of old text)

She used spinach, burrage, buglosse, endiffe, suckery, coleflowers, sorrel, marygold leaves, water cress, leeks, sporragus, rocket and alexanders

Her method was to - chop the leaves fine and set them on a chafin dish of coales with butter and vinegar. Season with sinamon, ginger, sugar and a few parboyled currans; garnish it withall with hard boiled eggs cut into quarters and serve it upon sippets

LOCAL MARFONA
10 Perlb

Carrot Croquettes

Boil 6 carrots until tender, drain and mash. Add seasoning to taste. Make a thick white sauce with a spoonful of cornflour, a knob of margarine and a cup of milk. Add the sieved carrot, leave until cold then shape into croquettes. These can be like thick biscuits or rolled like short, fat sausages. Roll in oatmeal and fry in deep, hot fat. Drain well and serve.

Potatoes can be substituted for the carrots to make potato croquettes

Fidgety Pie

Peel and slice 2 onions, 1 apple and 3 medium potatoes. Line a pie dish with pastry and put half of the sliced potatoes in the bottom. Cover with a layer of onions and a layer of apples. Shake in a teaspoon of sage, plus a pinch of salt and pepper. Half cover with stock. Place 1lb (450g) sliced and diced bacon on top. Sprinkle with 1oz (25g) sultanas and cover with the remainder of the potatoes. Put a pastry crust on the top and bake for 1½ hours in a hot oven.

Chesterfield Cheese and Vegetable Casserole

Peel and dice 6 medium potatoes, 2 carrots and 1 small turnip. Place in a pan of water that barely covers the diced veg. Bring to the boil and simmer for 5 minutes. Drain and put into a casserole dish with 12 sliced spring onions. Melt 2 oz (50g) butter in a pan and make a thick sauce with 2 tablespoons flour and ½ pint (275ml) milk. Add 2 egg yolks, 3oz (75g) cheese, salt and pepper to taste. Whisk the 2 egg whites until stiff. Fold into the sauce then pour the sauce over the vegetables. Place the casserole in a moderate oven for 25 minutes.

Gardener's Pie

Heat 3 tablespoons of oil in a large pan, add 2 peeled, chopped onions and 3 cloves of crushed garlic. Cook gently for four minutes, then add 2lb (900g) courgettes cut into slices, 1lb (450g) chopped tomatoes, 2 tablespoons tomato puree, 3 or 4 basil leaves, salt and pepper and cook for a further 4 minutes. Turn into an ovenproof dish and top with a mixture of 3oz (75g) fresh breadcrumbs, 2oz (50g) grated cheese and 2oz (50g) chopped nuts. Spread evenly and bake in the oven for 30 minutes.

top and middle left: Local grown vegetables are widely available in seaason
left: Collect fresh vegetables to make a gardeners pie
far left: Local grown Marfona potatoes

Meaty Main Courses

Making a hash of it!

The problem of how to turn left overs from one meal into another has tested cooks for hundreds of years. The thrifty re-use of left-overs has long shored up our larders, creating homely recipes like cottage pie, and bubble and squeak.

In many instances, the easy answer was to prepare a 'hash' – a concoction of mixed up meat, vegetables, gravy and sauce. The word comes from the Old French *hacher* meaning to chop or mince.

We talk about making a hash of something. This story is a prime example – Ash Wednesday is the first day of Lent, and was a solemn occasion deriving its name from the ancient practice of blessing the ashes. The priest used the occasion to remind his congregation that they too must one day return to ashes. However, it was said that many women ignoring the religious significance of the day called it Hash Wednesday and made beef hash for the family dinner

Beef Hash

Technically hash is any finely chopped ingredients mashed together into a course, chunky paste, then cooked. Beef hash could be the left over roast beef or a tin of corned beef. In the old days you would chop or mince everything together, but now it's far easier to put the left-over cold meat in a food processor along with 1 onion, 8oz (225g) cooked potatoes, 2oz (50g) breadcrumbs, 1 tablespoon chopped parsley, a twist of pepper and salt. When the meat is quite fine, tip

The problem of how to turn left-overs from one meal into another has tested cooks for hundreds of years

everything into a bowl and divide into 6 or 8 equal portions, roll each, then flatten and coat in breadcrumbs. Fry them in oil or fat, turning to make sure the hash is golden brown.

Bubble and Squeak

When people ate Sunday roasts with all the accompanying vegetables, little of such a feast went to waste. What was left over would be served on Monday to make that ridiculously named dish 'bubble and squeak'. The name is onomatopoeic, from the hissing and squeaking noise it makes when frying.

A 19th century recipe calls for slices of cooked meat covered with chopped cabbage, onion and other left-overs from the previous day. Combined together this is then flattened and fried until brown and crisp on both sides. It is then stirred with a fork until the crispy bits are incorporated into the whole, then fried again. When both sides are brown it is again stirred up with a fork until the bubble and squeak is full of crispy brown bits.

Monday Pie

When washday took up the whole of Monday, with no ready-meals to hand, dinner had to be quickly prepared.

Mince 8oz (225g) cooked meat and mix with a teacup of breadcrumbs, a finely chopped onion, the grated rind of half a lemon, salt and pepper. Pour over about ½ pint (275ml) of gravy or sufficient to make the mixture fairly moist. Grease a pie dish and line it with slices of tomato, fill up with the meat mixture and put more tomatoes on top. Cover with a dish or foil and bake for 30 minutes.

When washday took up the whole of Monday, and no ready meals to hand, dinner had to be quickly prepared (Bakewell Old House Museum)

Nadger's Pie

Nadger is an old Derbyshire name, origin unknown, but just ask them in Clowne, which is where this recipe comes from.

Melt a knob of dripping fat (lard or oil can be substituted) and fry 1 diced onion. Sprinkle over 1 teaspoon flour and enough stock to make a sauce. Add ½lb (225g) chopped or minced game meat, 1 chopped tomato, salt and pepper to taste. Stir over a low heat to blend well. Transfer to a greased oven dish. Cover with mashed potatoes and brown in a moderate oven for 30 minutes. Serves one nadger and his wife.

Derbyshire Savoury Pudding

Rather like the Yorkshire pudding, this Derbyshire Pudding is a savoury accompaniment. For poorer families that were usually rather large, it was always served with gravy before the meat course, because it helped to fill them up and eke out a small amount of meat.

Put 2 cups breadcrumbs and 1 cup oatmeal in a basin and cover with 1 pint (570ml) milk. Leave for 10 minutes, then beat in two eggs. In another basin, mix 2 cups plain flour, 1lb (450g) minced onions, 1 teaspoon minced sage, pepper and salt, then add to the batter and beat well. Bake in a greased tin for 45 minutes or until crisp and brown, then serve with your Sunday roast.

Inky Pinky

I have no idea where this name came from. It might appear more tempting if I could only get that old rhyme out of my head, you know the one – *'inky pinky, pen and inky, who made that big stinky'.*

Chop up an onion. Put in a pan with pre-cooked carrots and slices of left over, cold meat. Add salt, pepper and stock thickened with a little flour. Season with ketchup if liked. Make sure it is thoroughly heated, spoon onto a plate and serve with a border of mashed potatoes.

Stuffed Marrow

Pour a tablespoon of oil in a pan and throw in 1 finely chopped onion, a clove of garlic (optional) then 1lb (450g) minced meat. When the meat has turned colour and begun to brown, turn off the heat and add 1 cup of breadcrumbs, a tablespoon torn parsley, salt and pepper, a couple of bay leaves (optional) and 1 egg to bind. Cut one medium sized vegetable marrow in half lengthwise. Scoop out all the seeds and fill the cavity with the meat mix. Fasten the two halves back together and wrap in foil before placing in a pre-heated moderate oven for 1 hour.

Mystery Batter Pudding

If you want to keep the contents of your puddings and pies a secret, try this mystery batter pudding. Mix together ½lb (225g) chopped or minced cooked meat with any left over, chopped vegetables. Put in a greased pie dish and season well. Whisk 2 eggs, add ¼lb (110g) flour and ½ pint (275ml) milk. Beat well together. Pour over the meat and vegetables, and bake for half an hour.

Cut a marrow in half lengthwise
Scoop out the seeds
Mix minced meat, breadcrumbs, onion
and parsley – fry until it's turned colour,
then fill the marrow cavity

Potted Meat

Cut up 1lb (450g) beef steak and put in a pan with ¼ cup water, 2 cloves, 4 peppercorns, 1 teaspoon salt, ½ teaspoon pepper, a pinch of mace and cayenne. Cook gently for half an hour or until tender, then put through a mincer twice. Beat in 12oz (350g) butter and when thoroughly mixed, put in pots and seal with a layer of melted butter. To make the meat go further, a more economical version can be made with the addition of 2 slices of white, crustless bread. Ideal on sandwiches.

To make potted meat, take a slice of lean beef steak, cook gently, mince twice and pot

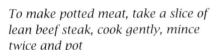

Ham and Tongue

No high tea, wedding tea, funeral tea or garden party would have been without ham and tongue which would be freshly sliced from the whole.

The flavour of a traditional ham whether boiled or baked is far superior when cooked on the bone. The raw ham needs soaking overnight to remove the salt used in the curing process. It may be necessary to drain off the water then recover the ham with more cold water. Bring to the boil and simmer gently for five minutes then drain off this water and throw it away too. If boiling the ham, add 1 pint (570ml) fresh hot water to which is added 1 tablespoon vinegar, 4 cloves, 6 peppercorns and 1 bay leaf. Cover and bring to the boil. Simmer 25 minutes per lb.

If baking the ham, originally it would have been encased in a flour and water crust, but now place it in a parcel of tin-foil in a baking tin and cook in a pre-heated slow oven for 20 minutes per lb (450g). Twenty minutes before cooking time is complete, take it from the oven and carefully remove the skin leaving a layer of fat. Mix up ½ cup of brown sugar and a teaspoon of mixed spices, pour this over the ham and rub into the fat, or coat it with honey and sprinkle on a teaspoon of mixed spices. Score the fat layer with a knife to form a diamond pattern and stud a clove into each diamond shape. Turn the oven to hot, return the ham and cook for the last 20-35 minutes until gold-brown. Eat hot or cold.

Put a 4lb (1.8kg) salted tongue to stand in cold water for several hours or preferably overnight. Drain off the water then recover the tongue with more cold water. Bring to the boil and simmer gently for five minutes. Remove from the heat and throw this water away. Add 1 pint (570ml) fresh hot water to which is added 1 tablespoon vinegar, 4 cloves, 6 peppercorns and 1 bay leaf. Cover and bring to the boil. Simmer 25 minutes per lb. When cooked, remove the tongue, skin, take off bones and root ends, and roll the tongue into a mould or cake tin. A tight fit ensures a professional result. Boil the stock until it's reduced to ¼ pint then strain over the tongue. Put a saucer and weight on top. Leave until firm and cold, then turn out. The stock will have formed a glaze which helps to keep the tongue moist. Slice when cold.

Jane Mosley's hand written recipe from 1690

To Roast a Neates Tongue on the French Fashion (translation of old text)

Chop sweet hearbes fine, with a Peece of raw apple, season it with pepper, Ginger and the yolke of a new Laid egge chopt small to mingle among it. Then stuffe it well with that farcing and so roast it. The sawce for it is verjuyce butter and the juyce of a lemmon and a little nutmegge. Let the tongue lye in the sawce when it goeth to the table. Garnish your dish as you thinke fittest or as you are furnisht.

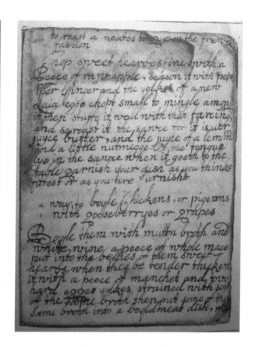

A copy from a page of Jane Mosley's 1690 cookery book – To Roast a Neates Tongue, and A Way to Boyle Chickes or Pigeons with Gooseberryes or Grapes

To cook oxtail

From tongue to tail

Joint an ox tail and put it in a pan with 4 pints (2.25ltr) of water, pepper and salt. Let the pan come to the boil and then simmer for three or four hours, when the water will be reduced. Add sliced onions, carrots, celery and turnips – swede and parsnips are optional. There must be sufficient liquid to cook the vegetables, if not, add a little more water or stock and let it cook for another half an hour. Make up a batch of dumplings (see recipe). Spoon these onto the surface and cook for a further half an hour.

Occasionally in old recipes, dumplings were made of small pieces of bread dough, about the size of walnuts which would be dropped into the broth or stew until they swelled up.

left: Put the oxtail, herbs and vegetables in a pan and cook gently for several hours

The Derby Ram

Derbyshire has been a sheep rearing district for hundreds of years and the ram is Derbyshire's mascot. It's the name of the football team, the radio station, and an ancient ballad called *The Derby Tup* (another name for the ram) which was often acted out by the 'mummers' around Christmas time.

Sheep rearing also had its superstitions. If you saw the first lamb of Spring facing you, it signified a diet of meat for the coming year and the money to afford it. If you saw the lamb's tail first, you'd be hard pushed to afford anything during the coming year. On the same theme, if the first butterfly you saw in Spring was white, you would eat white bread for the rest of the year. Conversely, a brown butterfly meant brown bread, traditionally associated with poverty.

Lamb is probably at its best in the Spring when the youngest lamb is available. Three to twelve month old lamb is tender to eat with a delicate flavour and its flesh is fine grained, velvety and pinkish/red in colour. Hogget is 1-2 year old lamb. The flesh is medium grained and red in colour. Mutton is 2 years and older. It's very tasty and somewhat firmer than lamb.

High Peak Braised Lamb Shank with Ale

This is the quintessential Derbyshire Lamb recipe. Throughout the year, sheep graze on the heather moors and grasslands of the upland hill farms in the Peak District, and at a time when most housewives brewed their own ale, it was regularly used for braising in preference to water.

In a large casserole dish make a marinade with ½ pint (275ml) ale, 4 garlic cloves, crushed and peeled, zest of a lemon, 10 peeled shallots, sprig of rosemary, salt and pepper seasoning. Add 6 High Peak lamb shanks cut off the leg, and leave to marinade for at least 30 minutes or preferably overnight.

Place the casserole in a pre-heated, moderate oven and cook for an hour. Turn the lamb shanks and add a tin of tomatoes. Return to the oven and cook for a further hour until the meat is soft and tender. Take four tablespoons of ale and add a spoonful of flour to form a thick paste. Add this and a tablespoon of chopped parsley to the casserole, heat thoroughly and when the sauce has thickened, serve.

above left: The Derby Ram – the sculpted model in Derby city centre by Michael Pegler.
left: Derbyshire has been a sheep rearing county for hundreds of years
right: Eyam annual sheep roast

Shepherd's Pie
also known as Cottage Pie

Mince llb (450g) cooked mutton and mix it with a cup of breadcrumbs, one small, chopped onion, a tablespoon chopped parsley, salt and pepper. Add sufficient gravy or stock to make a dropping consistency and put in a greased oven-proof dish. Cover with 1lb (450g) mashed potatoes, and put in a moderate oven until the top is lightly browned.

Rissoles

Mince 1lb (450g) cooked mutton and mix with ½lb (225g) mashed potatoes, 1 teaspoon finely chopped parsley, salt and pepper to taste. Moisten with 3 tablespoons gravy or stock and one beaten egg. Shape into balls, coat with beaten egg, cover with breadcrumbs and fry a nice brown.

Mutton Loaf

Mince llb (450g) raw mutton and mix with a cup of breadcrumbs, a cup of cooked spaghetti or macaroni, a small, chopped onion, a tablespoon chopped parsley, 1oz (25g) melted dripping, salt and pepper. Add an egg and sufficient gravy to bind stiffly. Put in a greased pudding basin, cover with greased paper and steam for two hours. Turn out and pour hot tomato sauce over to serve.

Sheep's Pluck

The cheaper cuts of meat make your money go further, but why do their names sound so unappetizing? Offal is the bits like heart, kidney and liver. Pluck is the liver attached to the windpipe and lungs, often referred to as lights because of their light weight. I used to buy pluck regularly and cook it for my dogs. They loved it, but last century it was a delicacy enjoyed by many families.

Cut the liver and lights into thin slices, and put them in a pie dish with a few slices of cut up bacon. Cover with a layer of onion and sliced potato. Sprinkle over chopped sage, mixed herbs, pepper and salt. Pour over a cup of water and cover with a piece of greaseproof paper. Cook in a pre-heated moderate oven for 1½ hours.

Derbyshire Haggis

Having noticed that the resilience of the sheep's stomach resisted all attempts at boiling, what was more natural than to stuff the stomach with a meat and cereal mixture.

Boil 8oz (225g) sheep's liver in water for 20 minutes, drain but retain the liquid, then mince with 2 onions. Brown a cup of oatmeal by tossing quickly in a frying pan over a high heat. Combine the liver, onions and oatmeal with 4oz (110g) suet, and enough of the retained liver liquid to form a stiff paste. Season with salt and pepper and stuff into the sheep's stomach (or a greased basin covered with greaseproof paper). Steam for two hours before serving with the traditional Scottish accompaniment of neaps and tatties.

Hog roast

Killing a pig

People used to rear pigs in the back yard. The family pig was fed on a mix of potato peelings, left over slops and barley meal. The children would be sent out to collect sow thistle, dandelions and snails for the pigs supper

When a pig was butchered it took place in the back-yard, but the task of killing and the subsequent preparation of the meat was carried out with the help of a few superstitions. The pig, like all beasts was traditionally only killed at the waxing of the moon as the moon in its growing stage was believed to result in meat that grew or at least didn't shrink in the cooking. As with other new-moon beliefs, in animal husbandry the notion of size was also translated into good and bad.

Pigs that were killed between 8 and 10 o'clock in the morning were believed to weigh more and be in better condition than they would if killed later in the day. After butchering, the helpers would receive parts. It was neighbourly to send a dish of pig-fare to a friend but on no account should the dish be washed before returning or it was believed the bacon would not cure. Traditionally, pork was only eaten when there was an R in the month, but that was in the days before refrigeration.

Sorting facts from fantasy, pork should be pale pink in colour and slightly marbled with small flecks of fat. There should be a good layer of firm white fat with a thin elastic skin (rind) which can be scored before roasting to provide crackling. All cuts of pork are normally tender, as pigs are slaughtered at an early age. Pork used to be well-cooked if not overcooked due to the danger of the parasite trichina. This no longer applies, and it is now recommended that the meat is cooked less to keep it moist and tender.

Pigs in Blankets

We couldn't leave this section without a mention of this most incongruously named dish. It is hard to imagine what could have inspired the name, but the reality is that this dish is actually a medium sized potato with a sausage threaded through a hole in the middle. To do this, take a medium sized potato, use an apple corer to make a hole through the potato, then feed in a sausage. Bake the potato in its jacket in the usual way in a moderate oven for an hour and when done, wrap a rasher of bacon round the outside to complete the cooking.

Mock Cutlets

Mince the remains of cold meat. Mix with the equal amount of bread-crumbs, flavour with herbs to taste, salt and pepper. Moisten with stock or gravy and form into the shape of cutlets. Dip these first into beaten egg, then breadcrumbs and fry until both sides are golden brown.

Mock Dishes

Mock dishes were introduced to make the best of restricted foods and encourage resourcefulness. Fake dishes mocked the luxury produce. Mock crab was made from powdered egg, cheese and salad cream; mock duck from sausage meat, onion and grated apple, and mock salmon from powdered eggs and tomato sauce. Bread, mashed with parsnips, a little sugar and some essence of banana made what passed as 'mashed bananas'.

Artistry was definitely at work when preparing mock goose. Mix a pint of breadcrumbs, ½lb (225g) minced liver, ¼lb (110g) suet, a tablespoon chopped parsley, ½ tablespoon chopped sage, ½ tablespoon chopped thyme, a little grated lemon rind, an egg and a little milk. When well mixed, form into the shape of a goose carcass. Cover with a layer of mashed potatoes and sculpt to look like the real thing. Cook long and carefully in a casserole or stewpot, crisping the outside layer of potato to resemble skin.

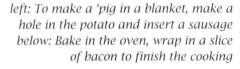

left: To make a 'pig in a blanket, make a hole in the potato and insert a sausage
below: Bake in the oven, wrap in a slice of bacon to finish the cooking

Chicken with wine and Mushrooms

Chicken with Wine and Mushrooms

Make a marinade with 2 wine glasses of white wine, (that home made dandelion wine that's not quite up to the standard of chablis is ideal), 2 finely chopped shallots, 4-6oz (100-175g) mushrooms, 2-3 tablespoons olive oil, a bouquet garni, salt and freshly ground pepper. Skin and slice up a chicken so that you have four pieces of breast and two thigh joints, and lay them in the marinade for 2-4 hours.

Because chickens are now not usually sold with the giblets – although turkeys are – make the stock from a carcass, either raw or cooked. Break it up and put in a pan with a couple of bay leaves, 1 sliced onion and sufficient water to cover. Bring to the boil and allow to simmer gently for an hour or so to make a stock. Drain off all the liquid and allow it to stand so that you can remove all the fat which floats on the surface. The stock will set to a jelly and can be used straight away or frozen for future use.

When ready to cook the chicken, instead of using the oven, heat the grill. Take the chicken joints from the marinade, brush with a little oil and grill for about 6 minutes each side. Slide them off the rack and into the bottom of the grill pan, and spoon over the marinade, removing the bouquet garni. Return to continue to cook for another 10-15 minutes, basting well with the marinade. Add some of the stock and a thickening agent to the marinade before serving

Chicken Stock

Chicken stock should ideally be made from the giblets – neck, gizzard, heart and feet, if available. Fry the giblets with an onion until lightly coloured then add 2 pints of water, a few pepper corns and a bouquet garni.

Because chickens are now not usually sold with the giblets – although turkeys are – make the stock from a carcass, either raw or cooked, as in the previous recipe.

Chicken Paste

After making a meal of a roast chicken, pick all the remaining meat off the carcass and use the bones and skin to make stock. Pound ½lb (225g) cold chicken, 2oz (50g) ham, 2oz (50g) butter, ½ teaspoon pounded mace, ¼ teaspoon ground nutmeg, salt and cayenne to taste. Keep pounding until reduced to a smooth paste. (It's much simpler to zap it in a liquidizer for a minute). Put into pots and cover with clarified butter. Ideal for sandwiches.

Pigeon

The popularity of dovecotes goes back to the Normans, but these were not just for aesthetic reasons. Dovecotes or pigeon houses became a feature of many houses and farm buildings, and in the 17th century there were 26,000 dovecotes housing from 500 to 10,000 birds each. The whole of the structure was functional with inner walls lined with a honeycomb of nest boxes. There are examples at Melbourne Hall, Haddon Hall, Highlow Hall, Knowsley Cross near Longnor and Ridgeway Farm near Repton as 200 years ago the keeping of pigeons was the prerogative of the well-to-do.

Pigeons are resourceful winter feeders and in all but the most severe winter months, they keep their condition pretty well. They were an important source of fresh meat in the days when all animals except essential breeding stock were slaughtered in the Autumn. Pigeon pie would be a welcome change from salted food.

Pigeon Pie

Line a deep pie dish with pastry and reserve enough for the lid. Strip all the meat from 2 uncooked pigeons or 1 uncooked grouse (most of the meat is in the breast) and cut into neat pieces. Put a couple of tablespoons of seasoned flour into a bag, drop in the meat, fasten the bag

and shake. This will coat the meat. Cut up 2 or 3 rashers of bacon, 1 onion and 4oz (110g) mushrooms. Combine with the meat and spoon into the pastry case. Pour over ¼ pint (150ml) stock and place the pastry on top. Seal and decorate with pastry leaves. Glaze with beaten egg and put in a pre-heated hot oven for 15 minutes. Put a piece of grease proof paper over the pastry, lower the heat to moderate and continue to cook for a further 1¼ hours.

Boiled Squabs with Grapes

Put 2 prepared squabs (young birds) into a saucepan with stock and herbs. Bring to the boil and simmer for two hours. Thicken the sauce. Melt a dessertspoon of butter and a dessertspoon of sugar in a pan, toss in the grapes and pour over the squabs before serving.

Jane Mosley's hand written recipe from 1690

A way to Boyle Chickes or Pigeons With Gooseberryes or Grapes (translation of old text)

Boyles them with mutton broth and white wine, a peece of whole mace. Put into the bellies of them sweet hearbs. When they be tender thicken it with a peece of manchet and two hard egge yolkes strained with some of the same broth. Then put some of the same broth into a boyldmeat dish with veriuyce, butter and sugar, and so boyle your grapes or gooseberries in the dish close covered till they be tender, and poure it on the breast of your dish

Pigeon with Red Wine

First make a pigeon stock. Skin the birds, remove the breasts and put these on one side. Put the remainder of the carcass in a roasting tin and place in a moderate oven for about half an hour or until well browned. Transfer to a stew pot with two large carrots cut into chunks, two sliced onions and a couple of bay leaves. Scrape the roasting tin and add a glass of red wine to the juices, then transfer this to the stew pot. Pour sufficient water over the carcasses to just cover them, bring to the boil and simmer gently for 2-3 hours.

When dealing with pigeon and many game birds, most of the meat is in the breast, so after slicing the breasts off a couple of birds, slice through the thicker part to make sure the thickness is equal. Marinade them in 1 tablespoon olive oil, ½ finely chopped onion, fresh thyme and pepper. Leave for a couple of hours, then remove and wipe clean. Give them a quick blush in a pan of hot oil, then put in a hot oven for 4-5 minutes to finish off. Don't overcook.

Game

Derbyshire is rich in excellent quality game. Duck, rabbit and wild boar are available all year, but Autumn heralds the start of the wild game season. In September it's the start of the goose, partridge and teal season, then October is the time for guinea fowl and pheasant. Duckling and gosling are March to September. Quail is June to August. The game season for grouse, wild duck, hare, pigeon, snipe, widgeon and woodcock is from August - January/ February/ March, but Venison is May to October.

ame meat is highly nutritious, easy to cook and has a rich depth of

Derbyshire is rich in excellent quality game

flavour. It's the way to bring the taste of the countryside to your table. Game birds can be roasted like chickens, but as they have very little fat, it helps to cover the breast in streaky bacon to cook them.

The wonderful flavour of wild game is ideal for anyone on a diet as you can have all the taste but none of the fat or cholesterol associated with many red meats. Pheasant and partridge are particularly high in protein and low in fat, cholesterol and sodium, making them a healthy food choice. They also contain high levels of iron, Vitamin B_6 and selenium which helps protect cells

from damage caused by free radicals. Venison is high in protein, low in fat and has fewer calories than other red meats. Venison is also particularly low in saturated fatty acids and contains higher iron levels than other meats

Rabbit

Rabbits provided a good family meal and could be bought for a tanner with a penny back for the skin from the rag and bone man. Poaching was rife but carried harsh penalties if a man was caught with a ferret. Ferrets were put down the rabbit holes to flush out the rabbits which were then caught in nets over the entrance tunnels. Amateur poachers used a snickle which is a rabbit snare made out of pop-bottle wires. One old timer remembers a time when he caught a hare in a snickle, but knowing that the game-keeper was around didn't dare collect it.

"I walked past him empty handed and hurried home. 'Quick Martha,' I said, 'there's a hare in a snickle about twenty yards from the lane bottom, along that hedge and there's a keeper watching, so if you go blackberrying, I'll put thee on a belt with a hook and a slip noose. Put on a loose frock, slip this round the hare's neck, hang it on the hook and drop thee frock.' Accompanied by two noisy children and under the nose of the keeper, Martha took the hare and walked home with it under her frock."

If you didn't know a poacher, the greengrocer came round with rabbits hanging from his cart. A lady from South Normanton remembers how in the 1920's, when rabbits were in season, a man came round selling them at 9d each or he'd skin them for an extra 5d.

Stewed Rabbit

Skin, clean, and cut up the rabbit. Toss in a frying pan until golden brown. Put in a saucepan with a pint of milk, an onion, a few cloves, salt and pepper. Simmer for an hour. Thicken the sauce with cornflour and return to the oven for 25 minutes.

This mixture makes a great stew or could also be put in a pastry lined dish and topped with a crust to make a rabbit pie.

Eating Umble Pie

The privileges dividing the rich from the poor were never more sharply defined than when it came to who got the meat. Fresh beef, mutton and pork were infrequent luxuries on the farm worker's table. They worked hard and lived frugally. From the middle ages to well into the Victorian era, the principle diet of the working classes consisted of bread, cheese and ale. This simple fare was supplemented as often as possible by pot-hunting, because for centuries poaching was not a pastime but a necessity.

At the end of a day of deer hunting, the lords got the venison and the serfs got the offal, called 'umble' when applied to deer and this gives us the phrase 'eating umble pie'.

Umble Pie

Take a heart or equivalent weight in offal and cover with water. Add some vinegar and soak overnight. Next day, drain and cut into small cubes. Cut 4oz (110g) liver and 4oz (110g) mushrooms into cubes and combine. Toss in flour, put in a dish and part cover with stock. Cover with pastry, brush with beaten egg and bake in a pre-heated hot oven for ½ hour, then reduce the heat to moderate and cook for a further 1½ hours.

Jane Mosley's hand written recipe from 1690

To Make Umble Pye

To make an umble pye or for want of umbles to doe it with, a lams head and purttenance (the edible innards of an animal). It will eate so like unto umbles, as that you shall hardly by taste discern it from right umblesan umble pye. Boyle your meat reasonable tender, take the flesh from the bones and mince it small. Add suet, marrow, liver, lights and heart, a few sweet herbs and currans. Season with salt, pepper and nutmeg.

Derbyshire Cheese and Milk

They say cheese was first made by accident when a shepherd boy put his days supply of milk into a pouch made of a sheep's stomach. As he ambled through the hills with his sheep, the sun warmed the milk and the rennet in the lining of the pouch turned the milk into curds and whey. When the shepherd boy stopped for a refreshing drink he found he had food and drink. He drank the whey and ate the cheese and the idea caught on. It's debateable whether this is fact or fiction, but what is certain is that cheese making was well established by Anglo Saxon times.

By the time of the Napoleonic wars (1799-1815), all the Derbyshire farms and many cottages made cheese, and production in 1817 was 2,000 tons per year. This era of prosperity brought with it a period of farm building, and although some are earlier, many Derbyshire farm houses date from the 1820-50s. This was a time when milk production was converted into cheese in the farmhouse dairy, so the cheese rooms were an important part of the building. Because the whey was consumed by the pigs, the piggeries were situated nearby for convenience too.

The River Trent and its canal links were used for transporting the cheeses, with warehouses situated on the canal sides at Derby, Shardlow and Horninglow, and because Hartington at this time was an important crossing point on the River Dove, the village had strategic importance. It was also a principle coaching stop for travellers on the first turnpiked road in the county, so perhaps those hungry passengers were able to tuck into Hartington's cheeses, which even at that time were considered superior.

The advent of the railways and the first train that puffed slowly past cud-chewing cows boosted the cheese shipping figure to 10,000 tons annually and some local farmers grouped together to produce cheese on a co-operative system. An article which appeared in The Derbyshire Advertiser in November 1913 gives details of the formation and running of the Gratton Cheese Factory Association.

'The scattered hamlet of Gratton lies just outside Elton, six miles south of Bakewell. Farmers in the Gratton district in 1884 formed a co-operation to manufacture cheese – The Gratton Cheese Factory Association. The secretary of the association was a farmer named Mr Wright, and the manager was Mr Chandler who has the certificate of the British Farmers Association for Stilton Cheese, also a certificate for butter and cheese making. The number of prizes taken at agricultural shows within the county and in a larger field proves the success of the undertaking. Gratton cheeses bear an excellent reputation for high and even quality. Amongst the prizes awarded have been first, Royal Show, Derby 1906; first and medal Derby show 1908; third London show 1910; first Derby show 1911; first and second London Dairy show 1911; first and second London dairy show 1912.

Roughly speaking, it takes about a gallon of milk to make a pound of cheese, but this is subject to variation. Milk in Spring is richer in solids than in the Autumn time. The local Shorthorn is excellent as a cheese producer, although the milk yield from an Ayrshire cow gives the largest proportion of cheese constituents. From 4,000 to 5,000 cheeses are made in the season which lasts from April to late Summer. Cheeses are left to ripen for up to a year for the connoisseurs.'

With the railways came change. Most farmers decided it was more

Hartington Cheeses

profitable to sell milk direct to the towns and the old cheese presses with their vast great stones and wooden screws were left to rot in barns. The farmer took his milk to the local station by horse and cart, and the early morning gathering of farmers milk floats and the rattle of milk churns became a country characteristic.

Then an American named Cornelius Schermerhorn introduced mass production to Europe, opened England's first cheese factory at Longford on May 4th 1870 and within 6 years Derbyshire was operating ten cheese factories.

In 1875, the Duke of Devonshire helped his tenant farmers open a cheese making factory at Hartington, but in 1895 changes to the milk business caused the dairy to close. In 1900 it re-opened on the site where it still remains today.

According to Ron Riley of Hartington:

Local farmers were the instigators of the cheese factory, built to take the surplus milk in the summertime, but when large imports of New Zealand cheese were imported in refrigerated ships, they couldn't compete and the factory was closed and fell into dereliction. Then the Nuttall family, who had lost their farm in a Leicester village due to an outbreak of foot and mouth disease, moved into the village. They had previously produced Stilton cheese on their farm, and this knowledge enabled them to reopen the factory and produce Stilton. The first load of Hartington Stilton went to London the day it was finished then a fire destroyed the factory which, being a wooden structure meant very little could be saved. The smell of toasted cheese hung over the village for days and Mr Brindley the manager had rows of salvaged cheeses put in the field and sold them at 2s6d each. The boiler itself still stood amongst the ruins and a pipe line to this was run to a nearby farm building where within a week, they were making cheese again

The variety of cheeses is almost infinite and the subtleties of flavour varies with the type of milk, climate, vegetation and method of production. Hartington could be called the Derbyshire centre of cheese making, and at the Olde Cheese Shoppe next to the creamery in the centre of the village you will be amazed at the variety of cheeses on offer. Hartington sits at the head of Dovedale so what could be more natural than to call one of its creamy blue cheeses – Dovedale. It is also famous for its Derby which is a particularly distinctive cheese. It is semi hard, white and smooth with an open texture. When young the flavour is buttery and mild, but it strengthens as the cheese matures.

Derby often comes in a form called Derby Sage, which can look like a layer cake with three or four bands of green filling. These vivid green streaks are produced by flavouring and colouring the cheese with finely chopped sage leaves. Derby Sage cheese was first produced in the 17th century when sage juice was added to the curds to produce a marbled effect and subtle herb flavour. Sage has always been a herb valued for its health giving properties, but occasionally the juice is made from bruised and steeped parsley, spinach or marigold leaves instead of sage.

above: A milk advert early 1900s far left: Getting the milk to market in 1906 below left: Getting the milk to market in 1950

Hartington produces a distinctive White Stilton which is a moist young cheese matured for three weeks to produce an open crumbly texture and fresh mild flavour. But what Hartington is most famous for is its Blue Stilton, a semi-hard creamy white cheese tinted with yellow and richly marbled with greenish blue veins. There are only seven dairies in the world licensed to make Stilton, and it can only be made in Derbyshire, Leicestershire and Nottinghamshire to a strict code. Hartington is the oldest Stilton creamery in the UK with 10% of production being exported to over 40 countries.

Blue Stilton was produced at Hartington by accident when mould got into a White Stilton making a cheese that attained to the noble stature called blue, a condition much to be desired in semi-hard cheeses. Cheese will usually not turn blue on demand; it is a combination of several factors. Sometimes cracks will develop in a cheese if the acidity is a bit too high and there is more moisture than normal; spores will enter and the cheese will 'blue'. A likely cheese can be selected and aerated with long, stainless-steel needles so that the spores can enter and grow in the cheese. This happy accident changes the open-textured, crumbly cheese into something quite different. The mould which is a positive citadel of rapidly multiplying fungi, penetrates the structure of the cheese breaking it down until the texture becomes softer, buttery and smooth. The flavour changes from the normally nutty, silky taste to the pungent, subtly rich, strong flavour characteristic of the blue mould which tastes sharp on the tongue yet bland in the mouth.

Of all the blue cheeses with their fugitive hint of ammoniac decay, the finest is Blue Stilton which is referred to as The King of Cheeses. A mature 8kg (14lb) Blue Stilton requires 78 litres (17 gallons) of milk and takes four months in the making. These wheels of prime Blue Stilton are covered by a thick crust which is dark and wrinkled, and unlike the cheaper blue cheeses, a Blue Stilton should always be sliced into wedges from the top, never scooped out with a spoon. This ensures that the cheese does not go dry and crumble and the texture remains constant all the way through.

Potted Cheese

There is a great history of potted foods – potted beef, potted shrimps, potted tongue, potted cheese – they were all a clever way of stretching one ingredient with butter, seasoning and the addition of spices, particularly mace – then sealed under clarified butter. Where once the ingredients would be pounded by hand, just whizz them together in a food processor.

Many old recipes suggest using port with stilton to make a potted cheese, but the colour and taste is not nearly as pleasing as adding brandy.

Into a food processor, put 12oz (350g) grated or crumbled cheese, 3oz (75g) unsalted butter, ½ teaspoon ground mace, and a pinch of cayenne pepper. Beat until

smooth, add 1 tablespoon brandy, taste and adjust flavouring. Pack tightly into small ceramic or glass jars. The flavour will deepen over several hours.

Storing Cheese

As cheese contains living organisms, it must not be cut off from air, so it is better stored in grease-proof paper than cling-film. Blue cheese in particular should be wrapped because the mould spores spread rapidly, not only to other cheeses but to everything nearby. Rub the cut edge of cheese with butter to stop it going hard.

Cheese grated on a wet plate will slide off more easily and grated cheese will keep well in a screw top jar in the refrigerator. A sugar cube in the jar will keep it from going mouldy

Home Made Cream Cheese

Unless you possess a cheese press it is impossible to make semi-hard cheese at home, yet many people made cream cheese using sour milk or cream. Like butter, this evolved as a way of extending the useful life of milk and cream which was simply allowed to stand undisturbed until it began to coagulate. The liquid whey would then be strained off. A teaspoon of salt would be mixed into the curds which were poured into a thin muslin cloth and left hanging

up until quite dry when they would be ready for the table.

According to the writer Alison Uttley who as a child lived at a farm at Cromford, they made cream cheese from sour milk which was saved and hung in a muslin bag in a cold window to drain for a day or two. The resultant curd was flavoured with salt and pepper, then shaped into a square cake. It was then placed under a two pound weight for the night, wrapped in hazel leaves in extra muslin. Next day it was wrapped in a thick piece of white cloth and buried in the garden about a foot deep. It was left there for three or four days then dug up and eaten.

At Christmas they made this cheese and put layers of finely chopped sage through it, rather like the Derby Sage cheese produced at Hartington

To get the milk to sour and set quicker, yogurt or sour milk can be added, but the easiest and quickest way is to add rennet. This can be bought in liquid form from some chemists and health shops, or an organic rennet can be found in organic shops. It's amazingly easy and versatile, and produces a cheese which is remarkably similar in texture and taste to ricotta. It can be used in sweet or savoury dishes, and any recipe that calls for ricotta.

Making Cream Cheese with Rennet

Sterilise a large saucepan by pouring in a kettle of boiling water. Pour this out then add 2 litres fresh milk and a pinch of salt. Heat gently to blood temperature as warm milk sours quicker and the curd will taste less bitter.

Remove from the heat and add 4 teaspoons rennet. Stir well, then leave for 15-20 minutes until the curds and whey have separated and it has 'jellied'. Pour off as much whey as possible then scoop out the curds into a double piece of muslin or a jelly bag and hang up for about 3 hours to allow it to drip over a basin. Your cheese will then be soft, sweet and curdy.

If sweetened it makes a dessert called junket (see desserts), but the unsweetened cheese will keep 'sweet' for 2-3 days if placed in a covered basin and stored in the fridge. The flavour will gradually turn more cheesy which is better for savoury dishes. Serve it crumbled over vegetables like spinach; into omelettes or hot pasta. Use within a week. Cheese is such a versatile food it adapts to any flavour and enhances it.

Ploughman's Lunch

'You can do a hard days work on a chunk of cheese,' so they say in Derbyshire as they tuck into a *Ploughman's Lunch. 'It's one of the finest lunches ever devised, incredibly simple, rustic and plain, yet a meal that can be memorable, given the right conditions.'*

Order a Ploughman's Lunch in any village inn or pub and with a bit of luck you will get freshly baked, crusty bread, a generous chunk of cheese, a couple of pickled onions and a foaming pint of bitter. Whether it's named after the man who walked behind the plough or whether it's a meal to plough into is unsure.

far right: A Hartington Stilton
top left: To get the milk to sour, add rennet
middle left: Hang the curds in a piece of muslin to drip over a basin
below left: The finished cheese will be soft, sweet and curdy

Toasted Cheese or Derbyshire Rarebit

Taking slightly more effort is another favourite lunch dish.

Slice 4-6oz (110-175g) semi-hard cheese onto a shallow dish that will fit over a pan of boiling water (unless you have a bain marie). Spread 1 teaspoon mustard over the cheese, and pepper to taste. Pour over 2-3 tablespoon of ale or milk, cover and set on heat. Don't overheat. When it is beginning to melt, stir it well and as soon as it is all melted, spoon onto toast and serve immediately.

Cheese and Walnuts

A slightly more sophisticated luncheon dish.

Beat 4oz (110g) strong blue cheese with 1oz (25g) butter. Finely chop a stalk of celery and a shallot. Add I tablespoon chopped parsley, celery salt and pepper to taste, add to the cheese mix, then bind with a little milk or cream. Press the mixture into a pot or mould. Brown a handful of walnuts lightly in 1oz (25g) butter, sprinkle on a little salt. Turn the cheese out of the mould and arrange the walnuts on top. Serve with salad.

below: Chesterfield Savoury Twists named after the town's famous Crooked Spire

Pears and Blue Cheese

Peal and core four ripe pears. Mix 2oz (50g) blue cheese with ½oz (10g) butter and fill the middle cavity of the pears. Set on one side. Take 3-4 tablespoons cream/curd cheese, season to taste and whisk in a little milk or cream to make a pouring consistency. Pour over the pears and sprinkle with a dusting of paprika.

Egg and Bacon Pie

Make a pastry case. Beat 2 eggs add 1 tablespoon grated cheese, seasoning and ½ pint (275ml) milk or cream. Lightly fry 2 rashers of diced bacon and 1 onion. Turn into egg mixture and pour into the pastry case Bake 30 minutes in a moderate oven.

Chesterfield Savoury Twists

The twist in Chesterfield's famous Crooked Spire has made it a well known Derbyshire landmark, and the reason for the twist is credited to the devil. Apparently, in the form of a dragon, he just happened to be flying over Chesterfield and decided to rest on top of the spire. He had just wrapped his tale round it when a whiff of incense from below made him sneeze, and as the sneeze shook his whole body it distorted the tightly held spire. Another well-known version is that while he was resting there, he twisted round in a bow to a beautiful and virtuous bride as she entered the church. A more slanderous version is that he jerked round in surprise because the bride was a virgin. A less romantic version says that a blacksmith at the nearby village of Barlow made a poor job of shoeing the devil who lashed out in agony as he passed over Chesterfield and gave the spire a violent kick.

Not to be too pedantic, the truth is that the 15th century spire which is 228ft tall and leans 7ft 6ins to the south is due to the use of unseasoned timbers that twisted under the weight of the lead plate that cover it, but who is going to believe that when the other versions are much more colorful.

Like the town's famous crooked spire, these pastries have a definite twist and have been baked to an old Derbyshire family recipe since 1920.

Sift 8oz (225g) plain or self-raising flour into a bowl, add 5oz (150g) softened butter and either rub in with the fingertips or use an electric mixer until the mixture looks like fine breadcrumbs. Stir in 2-3oz (50-75g) grated cheese and 1 teaspoon dried mustard powder or a dash of cayenne pepper. Mix to form a pliable dough with 1 egg and about 1 tablespoon of cold water Use just enough water to bind, roll out and cut into strips 1" (25mm) wide and 6" (150mm) long. Hold one end down, twist the other and place on a baking sheet. Bake in a hot oven for 15 minutes.

Mornay Sauce

Melt 1½ oz (35g) butter, remove from heat and stir in 3 tablespoon flour; blend in ¾ pint (425ml) milk; return to heat and stir until boiling. Cook for two minutes, season and allow to cool before beating in 3 tablespoons grated cheese and a teaspoon of mustard. Mornay sauce is very versatile. Use it to coat fish, meat, vegetables and pasta.

Cauliflower au Gratin

Lightly cook the sprigs of cauliflower in salted water, drain and arrange in a dish, pour over the mornay sauce and brown under the grill.

Eggs Florentine

Poach eggs for three minutes; cook spinach and arrange in a dish, place eggs on top, pour over the mornay sauce, sprinkle with grated cheese and brown under the grill.

Haddock Florentine

Poach haddock for 12 minutes; cook spinach and arrange in a dish, place haddock on top, pour over the mornay sauce, sprinkle with grated cheese and brown under the grill.

clockwise from top left: Mix the sifted flour, butter, grated cheese, dried mustard and a dash of cayenne pepper. Roll out and mark into strips. Cut each strip and twist. The finished twists are left to cool on the baking tray

Macaroni Cheese

Cook macaroni for about 20 minutes until tender, drain well, toss in the mornay sauce, arrange in a dish, sprinkle with grated cheese and brown under the grill.

Milk Recipes

Every morning there was the clatter of milk cans as the milkman came round. He'd use one of his jugs to measure out the milk and pour it into the customers milk-jug which usually sat on the dresser covered with a white lace doyley. Many people had no means of keeping food cold in hot weather and as spoilage and waste was abhorred, there were many hints on what evasive action to take. To keep milk in hot weather, the housewife was recommended to scald it as soon as received. To do this, 'put the jug in a pan of cold water, and place it on the stove. When the water boils, the milk is scalded and in condition for keeping for much longer than if left unscalded.'

Jane Mosley's hand written recipe from 1690

To Make Blanchet Manchet in a Frying Pan

Take halfe a dosen egges, halfe a pinte of sweet creame, a penny manchet grated, a nutmegge grated, two spoonfuls of rose water, two ounces of sugar; work all stiffe like a pudding. Then frye it like tansey in a little frying pan that it may be thicke; frye it browne and turn it out onto a plate. Cut it in quarters and serve it like a pudding. Scrape on sugar

Beestings Cake

The rich milk given by a cow after calving is called 'beestings' It was much prized and yellow with cream, but it was not drunk. It was used to make a delectable pastry filling called Beestings Cake. According to Alison Uttley at their Cromford farm, a pint of beestings was put into a pie-dish with a pinch of salt and a little sugar, and placed in a cool oven to solidify. Currants were added, then this creamy curd was poured into a pastry case and baked. When cooked it was transferred to the dairy where it was kept to become ice-cold, then cut in wedges.

Rice Pudding

For anyone who had a slow oven, this is one of the easiest puddings.

Melt 2oz (50g) butter over a low heat, sprinkle in 4oz (110g) rice and coat with the butter. Add 2oz (50g) sugar, ¾ pint (425ml) milk mixed with ¾ pint (425ml) cream. Stir for a couple of minutes to warm the milk and dissolve the sugar. Transfer to a buttered ovenproof dish and grate a little nutmeg over the top (optional). Place in a slow oven and leave for 3–3½ hours. Stir every half an hour to separate the grains, but leave for the last half an hour to form a golden-brown skin.

Cheese Cakes

Warm a pint of creamy milk and add a teaspoonful of liquid rennet. Pour off the whey, scoop off the curds and strain through muslin. Put the curds in a bowl with 4oz (110g) butter, 2 eggs beaten with a tablespoon brandy, sugar and the juice and grated rind of a lemon. Line some patty pans with good pastry, then pour in the curd mixture. Currants can be added as an optional extra. Sprinkle nutmeg on the top (optional) and bake.

Pastry

All Grandmother's cooking was done on a coal-fired, cast-iron stove with an oven at one side of the basket grate and a 7 gallon capacity water boiler at the other. Regulating the heat was a matter of experienced guess work and in recipes, oven temperatures were described as slow, moderate or hot.

To simplify the cooking temperatures we will do likewise, so use the scale below to clarify.

What could be nicer than melt in your mouth pastry with a memorable rich centre? Sadly, wet fillings often mean a soggy pastry base, so when making pastry dishes that have a wet filling like stewed fruit or meat in gravy, cool the filling before putting it in the case. Alternatively, the pastry case can be baked blind.

If baking blind, roll out the pastry and line a pie dish. Anchor it down with a sheet of greaseproof paper filled with baking beans or any dried beans/peas. Cook for approximately 15 minutes, remove the beans and greaseproof and replace the pastry case in the oven for three minutes to dry out the sweaty surface. Fill as required.

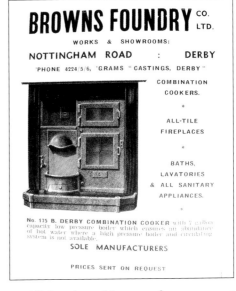

All Gran's cooking was done on a cast iron stove like this

	°Celsius	°Fahrenheit	Gas Regulo
Very slow oven	110-140	225-275	1/2-1
Slow oven	150-170	300-325	2-3
Moderate oven	180-190	350-375	4-5
Moderately hot oven	200-220	400-426	6-7
Hot to very hot oven	230-250	450-500	8-9

Savoury Shortcrust Pastry

Shortcrust pastry is what most people consider to be pastry, but there are a number of mouth-watering variations.

To make savoury short-crust pastry, mix 8oz (225g) sifted plain flour with a pinch of salt in a bowl. Add 4oz (110g) chopped up butter/white vegetable fat or lard, and either rub in with the fingertips or use an electric mixer until the mixture looks like fine breadcrumbs. Use just enough very cold water to bind into a ball. Chill and use as required.

Sweet Shortcrust Pastry

Sift 8oz (225g) plain flour into a bowl. Add 5oz (150g) softened butter, and either rub in with the fingertips or use an electric mixer until the mixture looks like fine breadcrumbs. Stir in 2 tablespoons caster sugar, then mix to form a pliable dough with an egg yolk and about 1 tablespoon of cold water or just enough to bind into a ball. Chill and use as required

To make pastry, cut the fat into small pieces, work it into the flour, add water and mix to a firm dough. When the pastry will leave the bowl clean, leave it to rest for half an hour

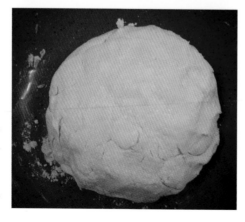

Flaky Pastry

Sift 8oz (225g) sifted plain flour with a pinch of salt into a bowl. Divide 5oz (150g) softened butter/ margarine or lard into 3 portions and rub 1 portion into the flour. Mix to a firm consistency with cold water, then roll out to a square shape. Chop the remaining two portions of fat into small pieces and scatter half of it over the centre portion. Visually mark the centre of the square then take one corner and fold it over so that the corner is in the centre. Do the same with the opposite corner, then the third so that you have something that resembles an envelope. Take the forth corner and close the 'envelope' with the fat inside. Seal the edges and 'rib' it. This means depressing it with a rolling pin at intervals to give a corrugated effect which will help trap the air. Roll the pastry to get a thinner square and repeat with the remainder of the fat. When this is all enclosed in an 'envelope' and 'ribbed' put the pastry in the fridge for thirty minutes to firm it up. If at any stage the pastry is feeling sticky and soft, put it in the fridge for thirty minutes before proceeding.

Altogether the pastry should have three foldings and three rollings, then before being baked it must be chilled as the contrast between the cold of the fridge and the heat of the oven makes the pastry rise better. Bake in a very hot oven for the first 15 minutes, then either turn off the power or lower the temperature to slow to finish cooking.

Suet Crust Pastry

Suet pastry can be used for both sweet and savoury dishes. Butchers used to add a lump of suet whenever you bought a piece of meat. If this wasn't rendered down and used as 'dripping' to spread on bread or toast, it was grated and used to make suet crust pastry.

Mix 8oz (225g) sifted self-raising flour with a pinch of salt in a bowl with 4oz (110g) suet. Add cold water by degrees until you have a workable dough ball.

Roll out two thirds of the suet crust pastry to line a pudding basin and keep a third for the lid. Change the quantities, keeping the same relationship of flour to suet to suit different sized basins. Your pastry case can be filled with a sweet or savoury filling.

Windberries which are the Derbyshire name for bilberries are native to the gritstone moors of Derbyshire where they thrive well on the peaty soil. Windberries sweetened with sugar are frequently served in a suet crust pastry.

Steak and kidney is a tradition savoury filling. Cut 1lb (450g) stewing steak and 4oz (110g) kidney into small cubes and roll in seasoned flour. Fill the pastry case and pour over 2 tablespoon stock or water.

Roll out the remaining suet crust pastry, wet round the edges with milk or water to act as a glue and place on top like a lid. Press the edges to seal, cover with a commercial lid or one made of greased paper or aluminium foil and put in a double saucepan for 3-4 hours to steam until cooked.

Dumplings

As an accompaniment to stews and casseroles your suet-crust pastry can be made into dumplings. Divide the suet crust pastry into six and form individual balls. Place these on the surface of a casserole for fifteen minutes. They will absorb some of the liquid and cook in the steam, so will be almost double in size when cooked. Spoon these out and serve with a ladle of stew.

Some people like to eat savoury dumplings coated in golden syrup, but for a truly savoury taste, add ½ teaspoon dry mustard.

Is food ready yet?

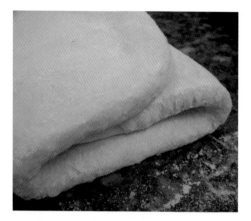

Rough Puff Pastry

Sift 1lb (450g) flour and salt into a mixing bowl. Cut 8oz (225g) butter/lard into thin slices and dust in flour, then cut into small pieces and toss them in the flour until coated. Add a little cold water with a squeeze of lemon juice, and work the ingredients to get a medium/firm dough that is not too sticky. On a well floured board, shape the dough into a fat rectangle with the length pointing away from you. Roll out with a well-floured rolling pin keeping the rectangular shape until it is about ¾ inch (2cm) thick or as thin as you can work it.

Visually divide the rectangle in three and fold the top third over the centre, then the bottom third over that making a fat, three tier rectangle of pastry. Turn so that the length is again pointing away from you, and dusting frequently with more flour, repeat the folding and rolling. This needs to be done at least three more times, but while working the pastry will get sticky or loose, so between each turn, put it in the fridge for an hour or so. Give it a final chill before rolling out and using.

Choux Pastry
(pronounced shoo)

Place 2oz (50g) butter with ¼ pint (150ml) water in a pan and heat gently until the butter has melted. Remove from the heat and add 3 oz (75g) plain white flour with a pinch of salt mixed in. Beat well then allow to cool for five minutes. Beat two medium eggs and gradually beat them into the mixture.

top right: To make rough puff pastry, the pastry must be folded and rolled at least three times.
middle and bottom right: Use the pastry to line a pie dish or cut into individual circles to line patty pans

Éclairs and Profiteroles

Choux pastry is used for éclairs and profiteroles, so to make éclairs put the mixture in a piping bag with a big nozzle and squeeze out 'sausages' of choux pastry. Cook in a pre-heated moderately hot oven for 15-25 minutes. Remove and make a slit in the side, if there is a small amount of uncooked pastry inside, either carefully scoop it out or return the tray to the oven and cook for a further few minutes in a low oven. Coat the tops with melted chocolate and when cold, fill with cream.

Éclairs are a tea-time treat but for a pudding make the choux pastry into profiteroles. Instead of piping a sausage of pastry, pipe small balls and cook as above. When cold fill with double cream and dust with icing sugar. Arrange them in a pyramid shape on a serving dish and dribble over chocolate sauce (see page 70).

Jane Mosley's hand written recipe from 1690, like all old recipes refers to pastry as paste

To Make Pufpaste

Take a quart of floure, a pound and a halfe of sweet butter, worke half a pound of the butter into the floure drie, betwixt your hands, then breake into the floure, foure egges, and as much fair water as will wet it, to make it reasonable like paste, then worke it into a peece of a foot long, strew a little floure on the table that it hang not to, then take it by the end, and beat it well about the board until it stretch long, and then double it, and taking both ends in your hand beat it again, and do so five or six times, then take the other pound of butter and cut it in thin slices, and spred it all over the one halfe of your paste, with youre thumbe. Then turne the other halfe over your buttered side and turn in the sides round about underneath, then crush it down with a roling pin and so worke it five or six times with your butter, then you may rowle it broad and cut it in foure quarters, and if it be not thin enough, rowle it thinner in round peeces, about the thickness of your little finger; then take a dish as broad as your peece of paste, and strow on a little floure on the dish, then lay on one peece of paste. You may put into it....... 'her choice of fillings varied from peeces of marrow and hartichoke bottomes, to apricockes without the stones'.....lay your other sheete upon this dish, and close it round about the brim of your dish with your tumbe; then cut off your round with a knife close by the brim of the dish. Then you may cut it crosse the brim of the dish like virginall keyes, and turne them crosse over one another, then bake them in an oven as hot as for small pyes.

When you see your paste rise up white in the oven and begin to turne yellow, then take it forth and wash it with rose-water and butter, scrape on fine sugar, and set it into the oven againe, about a quarter of an houre, then draw it forth, and serve it in.

Hot Water Crust Pastry

In a pan or microwave bowl, heat together ¼ pint (150ml) milk/ water and 4oz (110g) lard or white vegetable fat. When the fat has fully melted, pour the mixture into the middle of 1lb (450g) plain white flour with 1 teaspoon salt mixed in. Combine until the mixture forms a ball. Allow to cool slightly, then knead lightly until smooth and pliable. Reserving ¼ for the lid, knead and roll the rest to make a thick round. Set a large jar in the centre to form the shape, then lift and mould the hot crust pastry up the outside of the jar. Trim any excess pastry that can't be worked in, to achieve an even edge round the top. Ease the jar out carefully to produce a pastry shell which is used to make these delicious raised pork pies, veal and ham pies or a pie with a filling of your choice.

Raised Pork Pie

Mince 1lb (450g) shoulder or belly pork. Stir in a good teaspoon of mixed herbs, salt, pepper and 1 level teaspoon anchovy essence. Mix well then fill the hot water crust pastry case. Roll out the remaining pastry and take the jar previous used as the mould to cut out a pastry lid. Glaze the edges with milk or water to act like glue and place on top of the pie. Press the edges gently together, then crimp using your fingers in a squeezing motion. Make a small hole

in the centre. Cut pastry leaves from any spare pastry, dampen with a milk/water glue and arrange on top. Brush with beaten egg and bake in a pre-heated moderate oven for 1½ hours or until the pork is cooked. Allow to cool. In the meantime cover a chopped up pork bone or pigs trotters with sufficient water into which a couple of bay leaves and pepper corns have been added. Simmer for a few hours, then strain this stock into a bowl and skim off any fat. When cold this should turn to a jellied stock, but if it appears too thin, boil to reduce to about ¼ pint (150ml). Place a funnel in the central hole of the pie, then carefully pour in the jellied stock. The meat will soak this up so it is necessary to repeat several times. Allow your pork pie to be perfectly cold before serving.

The stages of making a pork pie with hot water crust pastry
1 – *Mould the pastry round a jam jar*
2 – *Ease it out gently and trim to neaten the edge*
3 – *Use pork belly*
4-5 – *Mince it fine, season and mix with herbs*
6 – *Fill the pastry case*
7 – *Put on the lid and decorate ready for the oven*
8 – *Boil a pig's trotter to make the jelly*
9-10 – *The finished pie - tuck in*

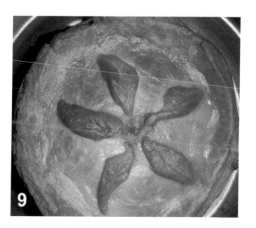

Veal and Ham Pie

Use two thirds of the pastry to line a 1lb (450g) loaf tin. Hard boil 2 eggs, shell and cut into halves. Cut 1lb veal and 6oz (175g) ham into small, neat cubes. Add ½ teaspoon lemon rind, salt and pepper. Mix well, then put ½ in the pastry lined tin. Lay the eggs across the top then fill with the remaining meat mixture. Pour over 3 tablespoons water or stock. Roll out the remaining pastry to form a pastry lid. Glaze the edges with milk or water to act like glue and place on top of the pie. Press the edges gently together, then crimp using your fingers in a squeezing motion. Make a small hole in the centre. Cut pastry leaves from any spare pastry, dampen with a milk/water glue and arrange on top. Brush with beaten egg and bake in a pre-heated moderate oven for 2-2½ hours. Allow to cool. Dissolve 1 level teaspoon gelatine in 4 tablespoon stock. Allow to cool slightly. Place a funnel in the central hole of the pie, then carefully pour in the jellied stock.

Collops and Pancakes

The period of Lent brought a significant change in the diet of the people because during this time it was forbidden to eat rich food. Eggs, meat, butter and other ingredients had to be cooked and eaten on the feast days of Shrovetide, leaving larders empty of all but the basic necessities. During these four days, the penitent people went to church to be shrived (thus the name Shrovetide) – to confess their sins to a priest in order to obtain sacramental forgiveness before the coming of Lent.

After Shrove Saturday and Sunday comes Collop Monday which seems to have almost disappeared from our calendar except for a few places in the North of England. The word *collop* probably originated in Saxon times and means a thin slice of food. My mother-in-law regularly served collops as a super dish, although in some areas they are called fritters. Depending upon the filling, they can be sweet or savoury, so use anything that can be thinly sliced and coated.

Emma's Collop Recipe

Make up the batter mixture using ½lb (225g) self-raising flour, ¼ teaspoon salt, 2 eggs and 1 pint (570ml) milk/water. Whisk well. Put a liberal amount of oil in a heavy pan or deep-fat fryer and heat to about 160 degrees. Take1 large potato, peeled and thinly sliced. Dip each thin slice of potato into the batter and when evenly coated, place in the hot oil. Allow to cook until crispy and golden brown, turning if necessary.

Pancake Day

Until the 19th and early 20th centuries, the Pancake Bell was rung in most parishes at 11a.m. on Shrove Tuesday. It told the villagers it was a holyday (holiday), an occasion for shriving at the church and time to start making pancakes.

Collops and pancakes would have been an excellent way of using up those rich foods pre-Lent, and although this is no longer applicable, eating pancakes on Shrove Tuesday is still practiced today, although

without the same superstitious ceremonies. It was believed that if the maid or the unmarried daughter of the house could successfully toss a pancake, she would be married within the year, but if she accidentally dropped her pancake on the floor or fire, she was carried outside and deposited in the midden.

The Winster Pancake Race

According to the story, when the Pancake Bell was rung on Shrove Tuesday, a harassed housewife, afraid of being late for the shriving service, ran to the church still clutching her pancake skillet. From this developed the idea of Pancake Racing, an old tradition which is believed to go back to the 15th century. The old lead mining town of Winster is the only village in Derbyshire to uphold this and although it's not known exactly when the Winster pancake race started, it has a written history which goes back to 1870.

Most people make pancakes for eating, so here is a good mixture that would also hold together well for the races.

Winster Pancake race

Pancake Batter

Break 2 eggs into a basin, beat and add 1 pint (570ml) milk. Mix ¼ teaspoon salt and 8oz (225g) self-raising flour, then pour in the egg mixture and beat well. Melt a small amount of lard or pour a dribble of oil in a frying pan and tilt the pan to coat the surface. The heat should not be too high. Add a ladle of batter and tilt the pan to get a thin, even coat. Ease round the edge with a spatula and when the underside is looking golden brown, turn the pancake over. This is the time to give them a toss, a traditional ritual in the cooking of pancakes and one that gets all the family participating.

Lift the cooked pancake onto a plate then sprinkle on sugar and orange or lemon juice. Although that's the traditional way, some people prefer them spread with jam, lemon curd or chocolate spread. Roll or fold before enjoying.

Pancake Batter Pudding

Grease a baking tin and half fill with the pancake batter. Roll 1lb (450g) gooseberries in sugar, drop them, well spaced in the batter, then bake for ¾ hour in a moderately hot oven until the batter is crisp on the top. Blackberries, apples cubes, or any other fruit can be substituted for the gooseberries.

Mystery Savoury Batter

It also works well with savoury filling, so chop up any left over, cooked scraps of meat and vegetables, add to the batter, then bake for ¾ hour in a moderately hot oven until the batter is crisp on the top.

Winster Pancake race

Oatcakes, Muffins, Crumpets & Pikelets

Another type of batter was used to make oatcakes, muffins, crumpets and pikelets. When every home had an open fire, these were a treat toasted in front of the blazing fire and served swimming with butter.

Traditional Derbyshire oatcakes are brittle unleavened cakes of oatmeal, but dating back to Bronze Age culture, they would have been made from barley-meal instead of oatmeal, and would have been called barleycakes. The batter would be cooked on a hot 'bakestone'. When cooked on one side they would be peeled off and while still damp and flexible, hung on a wooden rail to dry. When required for eating they were crisped before the fire, or fried in either lard or bacon fat till crisp. They were a tea-time treat, but for many lead mining families, along with cheese, they formed the basic diet when wheat was so dear and no bread was baked.

Remembering her childhood in South Normanton during the 1920s, Nora Jones said that every Monday morning a costermonger came round with his basket and bell shouting 'pikelets and oatcakes.' Similar recollections were made by Ron Riley of Hartington where Harry Hope, the oatcake man, sold his wares from a large basket over his arm. He always claimed that the fine flavour of the oatcakes was due to being baked over a wood stove, the bundles of wood having been carried on his back from Berrisford Dale by the side of the River Dove.

Derbyshire Oatcakes

Mix 2 tablespoons oatmeal, 2 tablespoons flour, 1 teaspoon baking powder and a pinch of salt with sufficient water to form a stiff batter. Grease a hot plate or frying pan, pour the mixture in and cook like pancakes for a few minutes each side.

Eat them fried with bacon and eggs or as a savoury snack with cheese and ham. Alternatively smother them in syrup or chocolate.

Although traditionally oatcakes were made from a dough containing no yeast or leavening, later yeast was added to the mix. Here is a subsequent recipe.

Mix ½lb (225g) oatmeal, ½lb (225g) flour and a pinch of salt in a warm bowl. Cream ½oz (10g) yeast and one teaspoon sugar together, then add ½ pint (275ml) tepid water – not too hot or it will kill the yeast. Pour into the dry ingredients and mix well to make a batter. Allow to stand for half an hour in a warm place to 'rise'. Grease a hot plate, girdle or frying pan, pour the mixture in and cook like pancakes for a few minutes each side.

Carsington Pikelets

Pikelets were the thin companions of the oatcakes

Put 1lb (450g) self-raising flour and 2oz (50g) sugar into a mixing bowl. Melt 1½ oz (35g) butter. Beat 3 eggs into 1 pint (570ml) milk. Make a well in the centre of the flour and pour in the melted butter and the egg/milk mixture beating slowly. When mixed, drop a spoonful onto a baking sheet and allow to spread. It should be thin and about 5 inches (12cm) across. Put under the grill until brown, turn and grill the other side. Cool. Serve toasted with butter spread on the bubbly side.

Place the rings in a heavy based frying pan, pour in the batter and cook gently. The surface will bubble to give the characteristic hole effect. Toast before serving, spread with butter and jam

Crumpets

These light, soft yeast cakes are full of small holes on the top, and are eaten toasted with butter and jam.

As well as a frying pan or griddle, to make crumpets you will need several metal crumpet rings. These can be poachette rings used for making 'neat' poached eggs or rosti rings for making neat rings of coarsely grated potato. The latest silicone egg rings are ideal for making shaped fried eggs, rosti or crumpets.

Heat 22 fluid ounce (625ml) milk to luke warm. Remove 5 fluid ounce (150ml) of it, and into this dissolve ½oz (10g) fresh yeast or 1 tablespoon of dried yeast. When thoroughly mixed return this to the remainder of the milk.

Sift 1lb (450g) plain flour and ½ teaspoon salt into a warm bowl. Make sure it is big enough as the mixture will swell to almost double in size Make a well in the centre of the flour, pour in the milk/yeast mixture and beat well to form a smooth batter the consistency of cream. Cover and leave for 30-40 minutes to rise. It helps to keep the mixture warm if the bowl is placed in a bowl or pan of hot water and covered.

Grease the crumpet rings liberally and place on a greased hotplate, girdle or frying pan over a medium heat. A girdle is a less common name for a griddle, and drop scones were often referred to as girdle scones. Pour in the batter to two third fill the rings. With a spatula move the rings to make sure they are not sticking, then lower the heat and cook until the bases are golden brown. The surface will bubble while cooking to give that distinctive hole effect. If the base is burning and the top is still liquid, either the crumpet is too thick or the heat too high. When beginning to set, turn over and cook for a further 3-4 minutes, but don't brown them because they need to be toasted before serving hot with butter, honey or jam.

This recipe makes approximately two dozen 2½ inch (60mm) diameter crumpets

Muffins

These light, circular, spongy yeast cakes are usually toasted and served with butter.

They were sold by itinerate men known as Muffin Men – as in the child's verse – *'Have you seen the Muffin man who lives down Drury Lane?'*

Muffins are made with the same ingredients and prepared in the same way as Crumpets but different amounts are used so that the mixture is a soft dough rather than a batter. You will need 4 inch diameter crumpet rings; girdle or frying pan although they can be cooked in a pre-set oven 375°F or Mark 5

Heat 15 fluid ounce (425ml) milk to luke warm. Remove 5 fluid ounce (150ml) of it, and into this dissolve ³/₄oz (15g) fresh yeast or 1½ tablespoon of dried yeast. When thoroughly mixed return this to the remainder of the milk.

Sift 1½ lb (675g) plain flour and ½ teaspoon salt into a warm bowl. Make sure it is big enough as the mixture will swell to almost double in size Make a well in the centre of the flour, pour in the milk/yeast mixture and mix well. Cover and leave for 30-40 minutes to rise. It helps to keep the mixture warm if the bowl is placed in a bowl or pan of hot water and covered.

When the dough is well risen, divide it into 12 even sized pieces, pat these lightly on a well-floured board in the shape of the crumpet ring and place one piece in each ring. Place in a pre-heated oven for 20-25 minutes, or on a hotplate, greased girdle or frying pan on a low/medium heat and cook on each side.

To serve, toast then pull them apart and spread thickly with butter.

Bread

Nothing smells more appetizing than newly baked bread. Most country housewives baked bread at least once a week, so here is a basic recipe.

Sieve 3lb (1.35kg) strong, plain flour and 3 teaspoons salt into a warm bowl or traditionally into a pancheon, one of those cream and brown steep sided earthenware bowls. In a smaller bowl cream together 1oz (25g) fresh yeast and 2 teaspoons sugar, then add 1¼ pints (720ml) tepid water. Make a well in the flour and pour in the liquid. Cover with a clean cloth and leave in a warm place for 15 minutes. It helps to keep the mixture warm if the bowl is placed in a bowl or pan of hot water and covered.

By this time, the surface of the liquid will be full of bubbles. Work the ingredients together and knead until you have a smooth dough that leaves the bowl clean. Put to rise in a warm place for about 1½ hours then knead again. Form into loaves and put into warmed and lightly greased bread tins. Each loaf should only fill half the tin as it will rise when cooking. Leave for a further 20 minutes then bake in a moderately hot oven for the first ten minutes, then reduce the heat to moderate for a further 30-45 minutes depending upon the size of the loaves.

Hot Cross Buns

There are many variations of bread, but one which deserves special mention are the hot-cross buns eaten at Easter. It was a general custom to bake on Good Friday as it was believed that the bread and the hot-cross buns, marked with a cross had miraculous powers. People not only ate them, they hung them from their kitchen ceilings to protect the household from evil for the year to come. They were used in powdered form to treat all sorts of illnesses and were believed to be particularly effective for stomach and bowel complaints, whooping cough, cholera and hiccups. Many farmers used it to dose ailing cattle. They would be as hard as a stone, and grated into water or broken into pieces that were soaked before use.

Good Friday bread and buns were said to never go mouldy. When they were needed, a few cobwebs would not have put anyone off, as these were also considered to have medicinal properties.

Put ¾oz (15g) yeast and 2oz (50g) sugar into a bowl and moisten with a dash of warm milk taken from 1 pint (5670ml). Rub 6oz (175g) butter into 1½lb (675g) flour and add a teaspoon mixed spice.

Reserve half the flour mixture, but combine the rest with the yeast mixture, 2oz (50g) sugar, 1 egg and the remaining tepid milk. Beat to form a batter then cover and leave in a warm place to rise for about an hour.

When it has risen and become frothy, work it up again. Add the remaining flour and 4oz (110g) currants and knead until it leaves the bowl clean. Cover the pan again and leave for an hour for the dough to rise. Knock it back again and shape the dough into small balls. Put them on a baking sheet and cut a cross on the top with a sharp knife. Brush them over with sweetened milk, then leave to rise. Place them in a moderately hot oven and again brush over with sweetened milk as they come out.

Puddings, Pies and Tarts

If you would have a good pudding
Pray mind what you are taught
Take two pennyworth of eggs
When they are twelve for a groat
Take the fruit of which Eve was
*   forbidden*
Well pared and well chopped at least
*   half a dozen*
Six ounces of bread (let Moll eat the
*   crust)*
The rest must be crumbled as fine as
*   the dust*
Six ounces of raisons from the stones
*   you must sort*
Lest they break out your teeth and
*   spoil all the sport*
Six ounces of sugar won't make it too
*   sweet*
Some salt and some nutmeg will
*   make it complete*
Three hours let it boil without any
*   flutter*
And then serve it up with sweet wine
*   and butter*

Courtesy of South Darley WI

Boil in the Bag Puddings

A pudding is normally something sweet which is eaten after a main, savoury course, as part of a meal. Early puddings were generally made from a basic mixture of meal, milk, sweetening and eggs; later spices and dried fruit was added to give plum pudding, figgy pudding, date pudding and currant pudding.

The resilience of the sheep's stomach to resist all attempts at boiling made it ideal for stuffing with these sweet pudding mixtures, rather like the savoury haggis is now. When Christmas cards feature the traditional Christmas pudding it always looks like a large football because of this method of holding it together while cooking. With no sheep's stomach or pigs bladder to hand, the mixture was tied in a cloth which was gathered into a bag and the bag pudding was invented. Boiling often took place in the tub that boiled the clothes on wash-day. Now we tend to use basins.

Stir Up Sunday

Traditionally, the plum or Christmas pudding is made on 'Stir-Up Sunday', the one nearest to St Andrew's Day (November 30th). It was called 'Stir-up-Sunday' because the Collect for that Sunday, the 25th after Trinity says *'Stir up we beseech thee, O Lord, the will of thy faithful people...'*

Although there is no mention of Christmas puddings, the day has always been synonymous with the making of the Christmas pudding which, in memory of Christ and his disciples, had thirteen ingredients incorporated into the mixture. Each member of the family in decreasing order of seniority stirred it three times while making a wish. Three was a pagan luck-bringing number, later linked with Trinity and the Three Kings.

The Christmas Pudding

There is a legend that one Christmas Eve a medieval king found himself deep in the forest where he came across a woodman's cottage. He knocked on the door and asked for food and shelter. The woodman willingly gave him shelter, then combined all the food he had and the result was a sticky mixture of chopped suet, flour, eggs, apples, dried plums (prunes), ale and sugar. With no pig's bladder to hand, the mixture was boiled in a cloth and the bag pudding was invented. The name 'plum pudding' continued to be used even when people used raisins, currants and sultanas instead of prunes.

This recipe has 18 ingredients, not the traditional 13, and is delicious, but who's counting!

Combine:
  4oz (110g) flour
  2oz (50g) breadcrumbs
  4oz (110g) shredded suet
  4oz (110g) grated apple
  1 small grated carrot
  4oz (110g) sugar
  4oz (110g) blanched almonds
  4oz (110g) chopped prunes or
      dried apricots
  2oz (50g) mixed peel
  1lb (450g) mixture of currants,
      raisins and sultanas
  1 teaspoon mixed spice
  ½ teaspoon cinnamon

  ½ teaspoon grated nutmeg
  1 tablespoon golden syrup
  Zest and juice of 1 lemon
  Zest and juice of 1 orange
  2 eggs
  ¼ pint (150ml) ale, beer, stout
      or milk

Mix well and leave overnight. Next day, spoon into 2 medium or one large basin and steam or boil for 6-8 hours. To reheat on Christmas Day, steam for two hours.

Steamed Carrot Pudding

Mix together one cup flour, one cup breadcrumbs, half cup suet, half cup mixed dried fruit, a cup grated raw carrot, a level teaspoonful bicarbonate of soda and a teaspoon mixed, sweet spice. Turn into a well-greased pudding basin making sure it is no more than two-thirds full. Boil or steam for at least two hours.

With the introduction of ovens, puddings could be baked on a bread base or contained in pastry so they became known as pies, tarts or flans. By 1430 pies had become standard fare and could be filled with all manner of things, sweet and savoury or both combined.

Carrots make tasty savory
and sweet dishes

Fruit Crumbles and Cobblers

The cobbler is a classic English pudding, a close cousin of the crumble.

To make the crumble, sift 4oz (110g) plain flour and 1 tablespoon baking powder into a bowl. Rub in 2oz (50g) butter until it resembles fine breadcrumbs. Add 2oz (50g) sugar, mix well and spoon over the fruit.

For the cobbler, sift 4oz (110g) plain flour and 1 tablespoon baking powder into a bowl. Rub in 2oz (50g) butter until it resembles fine breadcrumbs. Stir in 4oz (110g) ground almonds and 2oz (50g) sugar. Stir in 3 fluid oz (100ml) slightly warmed milk and 1 teaspoon lemon juice to give a soft dough.

Crumbles and Cobblers can be used with all kinds of fruit – plums, damsons, rhubarb, gooseberries, blackberries and apples. Just slightly sweeten the fruit and cook to a juicy compote, spoon into an ovenproof dish, then pile the crumble mix or 6-8 generous dessertspoons of the cobbler mixture – each one a cobbler – over the surface of the fruit before baking in a moderate oven for 30 minutes.

The stages of making a blackberry and apple crumble

Bread and Butter Pudding

Bread is so versatile and this pudding is a lot more appetizing than it sounds.

Lightly butter an oven-proof dish. Place a layer of bread, buttered on one side, sprinkle with raisins soaked overnight in rum (optional), then another layer of bread and more raisins. Whip 3 eggs with ½ pint (275ml) cream and ½ pint (275ml) milk. Add sugar to taste. Use a knife to make significant holes in the bread, then pour in the egg mixture. When it has more or less all soaked in, place the dish in a moderate oven and bake until the top is crispy and golden.

Brown Betty Pudding

Peel, core and slice 1lb (450g) apples. Grate the rind of one lemon, squeeze out the juice and add to the apple with ½ cup water. Take 2 teacups of breadcrumbs, sprinkle on a tablespoon of sugar (or to taste). Into a greased pie dish place a layer of apple, sprinkle over half the crumb mixture, another layer of apples and top with the remaining crumbs. Dot the top with butter and bake in a moderate oven for ¾ hour

Mucky Mouth Pie

Not a terribly appetizing name until you realise it's from the juice stains left round the mouth after eating strong, fruity berries like blackberries, blackcurrants and bilberries. Alongside garden grown fruits like gooseberries and currants (the red, black and white variety not dried), the hedgerows might be called Derbyshire's wild gardens. Elderflowers, elderberries, crab-apples, rose-hips, rowan berries, blackberries, windberries (bilberries) are all available in the Derbyshire countryside and make excellent puddings, drinks, jams and chutneys. Just one word of warning, pick blackberries by September 29th – Michaelmas. This is the day when the devil poisons the fruit by spitting or urinating on them.

When preparing apples for a pie don't forget the old Derbyshire saying – 'Apple pie without the cheese is like a kiss without the squeeze'

The Apple Harvest

Apple trees have for centuries provided a bountiful harvest, and there are numerous recipes for apples, some coming under the heading of pippin like Pippin Pye.

It was believed that if the first rays of sun could be seen through the apple trees on Christmas morning, it meant a plentiful harvest. An old pagan custom that continued for

Apple Pie

many centuries was for people to go wassailing to apple orchards on Old Year's Night to ensure a good harvest. They would make as much noise as they could with tin lids and bird scarers to ward off evil spirits that may be lurking to damage the apple harvest, then one tree would be selected and after praying for a good apple crop, they'd sing wassailing songs, drink hot cider and pour some over the roots of the tree. Apples were incorporated into sweet and savoury dishes and it was customary to eat cheese with apples. There's an old Derbyshire saying – *'Apple pie without the cheese, is like a kiss without the squeeze'.*

Line a pie dish with shortcrust pastry. Peel, core and slice 1½ lb (675g) apples. Place in the pastry case, then sprinkle over ½ teaspoon cinnamon, ½ teaspoon bruised cloves, 1 teaspoon grated orange rind and 2 tablespoon sugar. Spray with cold water to distribute the seasoning and sugar through the apples. Cover with a pastry lid and seal the edges. Cook in a moderate oven for 35 minutes. Dust the top with sugar before serving – and don't forget the cheese.

Jane Mosley's hand written recipe from 1690

To Make Pippin Pye

Take their weight (the weight of the apples) in sugar, and sticke a whole clove in each peece of them, and put in peeces of whole sinamon, then put in all your sugar with a slice or two of whole ginger; sprinkle rose water on them before you close your pye; bake them and serve them in.

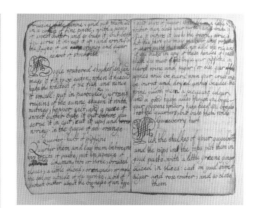

above: A copy from a page of Jane Mosley's 1690 cookery book - recipe for Pippin Pye and Quarter Tart of Pippins and Gooseberry Tart

Jane Mosley's hand written recipe from 1690

To Make Quarter Tart of Pippins

Quarter them and lay them between two sheets of paste; put in a peece of whole sinamon, two or three bruised cloves, a little sliced, orengado, or onely the yellow outside of the oarnge, a bit of sweet butter about the bignesse of an egge, good store of sugar; sprinkle on a little rose water then close your tarte and bake it.

Ice it before it goe to the boord, serve it hot. This tarte you may make of any puf paste or short paste that will not hold the raysing. If you bake in any of these kinds of pastes, then you must first boyle your pippins in calret wine and sugar, or your apples will be hard wen your crust will be burnt, and dryed away besides, the wine giveth them a pleasant colour, and a good taste also. Though you boyle your pippens tender, take heed you breake not the quarters, but bake them whole

Toffee and Apple Pie

(Courtesy of Thornton's the Alfreton based confectionary company)

Line a pie dish with pastry, but reserve a third for the lid.

For the filling, put 1lb (450g) cooking apples, peeled and cored into a pan and cook gently with a dash of water and 4oz (110g) sugar. Using a rolling pin break up 6oz (175g) Thornton's Toffee and scatter this over the cooked apple. Allow the apple mixture to cool slightly then place in the pastry case. Glaze the edges of the pastry with milk to act like glue and place the lid on top. Press the edges down firmly and trim off the excess. Crimp the edges and bake in a pre-heated, moderate oven for 30-40 minutes or until golden brown. Sprinkle with caster sugar and serve with cream, ice cream or custard.

Butterscotch Apples

A quick, no bake treat for all those fans of toffee apples

Peel, core and dice 4 or 5 firm eating apples. Melt 2oz (50g) butter in a pan and fry the apples very gently. Sprinkle on 2oz (50g) sugar then keep frying and gently tossing until the apples are tender and coated with a butterscotch glaze. Serve with a generous dollop of cream or ice-cream.

Lemon Meringue Pie

Line a pie dish with shortcrust pastry and bake 'blind'. Mix 2 egg yokes, ¾ cup of milk, 2 tablespoons sugar, 2 tablespoons breadcrumbs, juice and peel of 2 lemons. Pour into the pastry case. Beat the egg whites until stiff, then gradually add a tablespoon of sugar. Spoon this stiff meringue mixture over the pie filling and cook in a slow oven until the meringue is crisp and just turning golden.

Alternatively, use a meringue mix to make a base to hold other fillings. Spread the meringue mixture in a circle on a well-greased tray or parchment and build a wall of meringue round the edge. Bake in a very slow oven until crisp but not coloured and if not using immediately, store in an airtight tin.

Feeberry Pie

Feeberry is the old Derbyshire name for gooseberry. Origin unknown, but just ask the folks in Bradwell, which is where this recipe comes from.

Line a pie dish with pastry, but reserve a third for the lid. Put in 2lb (900g) feeberries – topped and tailed, 1 tablespoon water and sugar to taste. Roll out a circle of pastry to fit the top, put a ring of cold water round the edges so they will seal and cover. Prick the top to make a vent for the steam and bake in a pre-heated, moderately hot oven for 35 minutes.

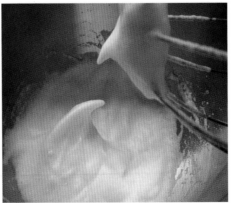

left: Beat the egg whites to form a meringue topping or a meringue case
far left: Young gooseberries peeping out of the bush, but no babies that were traditionally supposed to be found under a gooseberry bush

Gooseberry and Elderflower Flan

Line a pie dish with pastry, and place in refrigerator until needed. Put 1lb (450g) gooseberries topped and tailed, a few heads of elderflower – cleaned, and six tablespoons white wine into a pan. Simmer gently until the fruit is soft, then remove the elderflowers. Liquidize the fruit mixture then sieve into a clean bowl. Add 4 tablespoons of warmed honey, 2 beaten eggs, and a pinch of nutmeg. Beat well and pour into the prepared pastry case. Bake for about 40 minutes in a moderate oven until firm and golden brown. Serve chilled with ice-cream, evaporated milk or cream.

Rhubarb Pie

Line a pie dish with pastry, but reserve a third for the lid. Cut 1½ lb (675g) rhubarb into small pieces. Mix 3 tablespoons flour and 8oz (225g) sugar together in a bowl, and add a beaten egg. Beat thoroughly then add the rhubarb cubes. Spoon this mixture into the pastry case and make a lattice top with the remaining pastry. Brush with beaten egg, then bake for about 40 minutes in a moderate oven until fruit is soft and pastry is golden brown. Serve chilled with ice-cream, evaporated milk or cream.

Kick Pudding

There are many interesting fillings for your pies and tarts as this idea from Alison Uttley show. I also found the almost identical recipe in an old cookery book labelled 'kick pudding'. I image that's the effect of the rum, so I've adopted the name.

Line a tin with pastry. Make the filling by melting 4oz (110g) butter and pouring over 4oz (110g) sugar and 4oz (110g) currants. Add 2oz (50g) flour, a teaspoon of rum and some lemon zest. Mix well. Spoon into the pastry case and bake.

Jane Mosley's hand written recipe from 1690

To Make Goosebery Tart

Pick the stalks of your gooseberries and the pips in the tops. Put them in goode paste (pastry) with a little greene ginger sliced in slices; cast on good store of sugar and rose water, and so close them.

below and left: Freshly picked red currants and young rhubarb make delicious pies

Lattice Pastry Cases

Pastry cases were sectioned with complex patterns, each section filled with a slightly different coloured preserve and separated by a fine roll of pastry. This reflects a tradition that dates back to the medieval times when great importance was placed on the number of preserved fruits a household could produce. Colour was everything, so a simple apple cheese recipe would be adapted to produce shades from the palest green through amber to red. The multicoloured fruit pastes were then used to fill the elaborate sectioned pastry tarts with complex patterns.

In a simplified version, a basic two tone effect can be made with jam and lemon curd. Line a tin with pastry. Roll out the offcuts and cut slim slivers of pastry to section the case. Glue them in place with milk, then carefully spoon the fillings into each section. Make sure not to overfill or the effect will be lost.

Derbyshire Moorland Tartlets

Line 12 patty pans with good pastry. Hard boil 4 eggs. Allow to cool, shell and grate them. Cream ½lb (225g) sugar, ½lb (225g) butter. Add ½lb (225g) currants, a little grated nutmeg and the grated eggs. Mix well. Spoon into the pastry cases and bake.

Derbyshire Lemon Rice Cakes

Line 12 patty pans with pastry. Melt 2oz (50g) butter and pour over 2oz (50g) ground rice, 4oz (110g) fine sugar, 2oz (50g) raisins or currants, 1 beaten egg, ¼ teaspoon baking powder, juice and zest of a lemon. Mix well. Spoon into the pastry cases and bake for about 20 minutes.

left (top to bottom): Pastry cases sectioned with complex patterns were a popular way to show off multicolored fruit pastes
right: The Bakewell Pudding originated at The Rutland Hotel, which still stands in the heart of Bakewell

The Bakewell Pudding

For millions who have never visited Derbyshire or the old market town of Bakewell, the name is familiar through the Bakewell pudding.

The story of its origin dates back to the end of the 18th century and the kitchen of The White Horse, a busy coaching inn that stood in the centre of Bakewell. In 1805 it was replaced by The Rutland Hotel with its fine Georgian façade, and the first proprietor was a Mr William Greaves helped by his wife Anne, a family association that lasted almost a century.

Anne was well known for the wholesome fare which she served to coach travellers, local gentry and residents who included such famous names as John Ruskin and Jane Austen. Jane stayed at the Rutland Hotel in 1811 while writing Pride & Prejudice, using Bakewell lightly disguised as Lambton and Chatsworth House, her inspiration for Pemberley. There is every likelihood that she ate Bakewell Pudding.

The Bakewell pudding was a culinary mistake according to the most widely accepted account of its origin. Mrs Greaves asked one of her kitchen maids to complete the pudding she had started preparing, but the maid misunderstood, spread jam on the pastry base then poured a rich egg mixture over. The result was delicious and from then on continued to be made that way.

Apparently when Mrs Greaves had her will written up by a Mr Radford, the original recipe, which had become a regional and national favourite was included in her papers, but Mr Radford passed the recipe to Mr Bloomer, a Bakewell baker so that he could make and sell the genuine thing. Apparently the recipe is still in the firm's safe and Bloomers still bake Bakewell puddings to the original recipe. However, another contender is The Original Bakewell Pudding Shop, the premises of which for most of the 19th century was a confectioners. They not only sold the Bakewell pudding from these premises they claim to also have the

An image of Anne Greaves, the 19th century proprietor of the Rutland Hotel is displayed in the window of the original Bakewell Pudding Shop where, as this plaque proclaims, this delicacy has been sold since 1865

original recipe which was extracted from the kitchen maid. Both organisations prefer to keep the original recipe a secret, but although there are a number of variations, there are no mystery ingredients.

The Bakewell pudding is made in three layers – pastry, jam and a filling, a technique that goes back to at least Tudor times. The authentic Bakewell pudding is not a cake mixture. It has no flour, ground almonds or almond essence, but is more like a rich custard of butter, sugar and eggs.

The earliest dateable recipe for Mrs Greaves' Bakewell pudding is to be found in the hand-written notebooks of Mrs Thornhill of Great Longstone, dated 1863, now held in the Record Office, Matlock (11th recipe listed under 'Cakes – large').

top middle: Silhouette of Anne Greaves (1778-1853) by White Watson
left: The original Bakewell Pudding Shop
above: Bakewell Pudding recipes from Mrs Thornhills Recipe Book dated 1863

Bakewell Pudding

An authentic early 19th century recipe

Line a tin with puff paste. Cover the bottom with a layer of strawberry jam. Put ¼ lb (110g) butter into a pan and let it boil up. Skim it carefully. Beat 5 egg yolks and 3 egg whites with ¼ lb (110g) castor sugar. Stir into the butter, beat up together and layer this mixture on the jam. Bake until it is delicately brown.

Bakewell Pudding

Bakewell recipe

Line a pie dish with puff pastry, and spread over a thick layer of strawberry jam. Mix 4oz (110g) sugar and 4 egg yokes; add 4oz (110g) melted butter and a dash of almond essence. Whisk 4 egg whites and gently fold into the mixture. Spread this over the jam and bake in a moderately hot oven for 15 minutes, then turn down to moderate for 25 minutes.

To make a Bakewell Pudding, first line a tin with pastry and spread jam in the base. Spoon the mixture over the jam and bake

Buxton Pudding

Although similar to its Bakewell neighbour, this Buxton pudding doesn't have the same recognition or fame. Buxton pudding is to be found in the hand-written notebooks of Mrs Thornhill of Great Longstone, dated 1863, in the County Record Office, Matlock.

Line a pie dish with puff pastry, and spread over a thick layer of strawberry jam. Cream 2oz (50g) butter and 2oz (50g) sugar until light and fluffy, then add 2 well beaten eggs, 2oz (50g) bread crumbs and a dash of water if necessary. Spoon this mixture over the jam base and bake in a moderate oven for about 35 minutes.

Derbyshire Pudding

This is slightly more elaborate version of the early Bakewell pudding.

Line a pie dish with short crust pastry, and spread over a thick layer of jam. Cream 2oz (50g) butter and 2oz (50g) sugar until light and fluffy, then add 1 egg and beat well. Sift 3 oz (75g) self-raising flour and fold into the mixture adding a little water if necessary. Warm 1 tablespoon lemon curd, and pour into the mixture to get a marbled effect, but do not stir or mix. Spoon this mixture over the jam base and bake in a moderate oven for around 35 minutes.

Mincepies

A seasonal pie that only seems to be eaten at Christmas is the mince pie. To say the filling is mincemeat makes it sound savoury yet the mincemeat mix is extremely sweet. The reason for the name is because mince pies are descended from pies which contained a variety of meats as well as fruit and spices, and date to pre-Elizabethan times. These pies were very much bigger than the individual mince pies we eat today, oblong in shape and called crib pies because they were similar in shape to the manger in which the baby Jesus was laid. By the mid 17th century, the pies had become round, were known as mince pies and contained dried fruit and spices without the meat. There is just one savoury ingredient that is still used in remembrance of the shepherds of Bethlehem – the mutton suet.

Mincepies were originally also called 'wayfarers' pies as they were given to visitors during the Christmas holidays. It was thought to be lucky to eat twelve mince pies in twelve different households during the twelve days of Christmas to ensure a happy twelve months in the year ahead. And if that wasn't enough, mince pies had to be made in twelves to strengthen the charm and unsurprisingly, to make mincemeat twelve ingredients are mixed together.

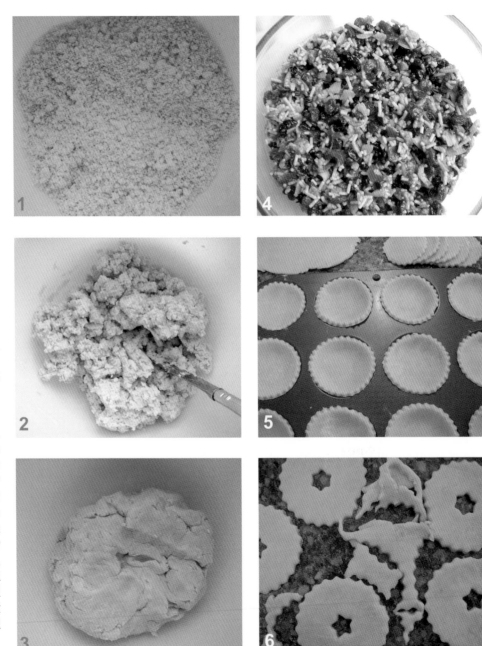

Combine 4oz (110g) shredded suet, 4oz (110g) grated apple, 4oz (110g) sugar, 4oz (110g) blanched almonds, 4oz (110g) mixed peel, 1lb (450g) mixed dried fruit, 1 teaspoon mixed spice, ½ teaspoon cinnamon, ½ teaspoon grated nutmeg, zest and juice of 1 large lemon, zest of an orange, 4 tablespoons brandy or rum. Mix well and spoon into sterile jars. Leave for at least 24 hours before using but the taste improves with keeping.

To make mincepies, line 12 patty pans with pastry, spoon in the mincemeat and top with a pastry lid, wiping round the edge to seal the pastry. Before placing the lid in position, cut a seasonal shape out of the centre of the pastry. Bake for about 20 minutes, dust with icing sugar before serving and don't forget to leave one for Santa!

Mincepies
1-3   *Make a rich pastry*
4   *Mincemeat used to be half sweet and half savoury but now has just one savoury ingredient added – the mutton suet in remembrance of the shepherds of Bethlehem*
5   *Line 12 patty tins with the pastry*
6-7   *Cut out a decorative lid*
8-10   *Star shapes make a seasonal lid*
11   *Add a bit of variety*
12   *Don't forget to leave a mincepie for Santa*

Summer Desserts

English gardens and markets overflow with delicious fruits in summer. When fruit is perfect it is best served raw and whole. The visual pleasure of a dish of firm, fresh fruit like strawberries, raspberries, plums, cherries and apples is matched only by its succulent taste. Soft fruit like strawberries and raspberries are traditionally hulled - stalks and leaves removed - then served with a dollop of cream, but for extra flavour coat them with a lip – smacking syrup.

Fruits like the red/black and white currants, gooseberries, rhubarb, damsons and blackberries are more palatable when cooked.

right: Fruits like these white currants
are more palatable when cooked
far right: Succulent apples
ready for picking

Summer Pudding

This deliciously easy, quint-essentially English cold pudding consists of a bread lining soaked with lightly cooked and juicy summer soft fruits. In my grandmother's cookery book it is called Hydropathic Pudding, so it was probably considered highly nutritious and easy to swallow for invalids.

Put 1½lb (675g) mixed fruity berries into a pan. Apples can be used but for extra effect the bread needs to be soaked in a strong red juice, so it is best to use a large proportion of jumble berries, the term for an assortment of berries. Add 5oz (150g) sugar and simmer gently until the fruit is almost soft. Cool and adjust the sweetening if necessary. Meanwhile cut the crusts off the bread. Make the crusts into breadcrumbs for later use. Mould the slices round the inside of a 2 pint pudding basin. Spoon the fruit into the bread-lined basin until it's half full. Put in another layer of bread, more fruit and finish with a layer of bread soaked in juice. Reserving 2-3 spoons of juice. Put a plate on top and weigh this down to thoroughly soak the bread. Chill overnight, then turn out just before serving. If any of the bread is uncoloured, paint on the reserved juice. Serve with cream, ice cream or evaporated milk.

Rhubarb and Custard Trifle

Wash, trim and cut 1lb (450g) rhubarb. Put into a pan with 3 tablespoons orange juice and 4 tablespoons sugar. Simmer gently until the stalks are just tender (about 8-10 minutes). Add more sugar if it is very tart, the acidity of rhubarb can be reduced by cooking in cold tea. Strain off all the excess juice and chill both juice and rhubarb in the fridge.

Make a rich custard. Put ½ pint (275ml) double cream and ½ pint (275ml) milk in a pan with a split vanilla pod and heat. Beat 4 large egg yokes with 4oz (110g) caster sugar and whisk in the hot cream. Return this custard to the pan over a low heat and stir constantly until it thickens. Remove from the heat, continue to stir for a minute as it cools, then strain through a sieve into a bowl and chill.

Take a plain sponge cake, break it into pieces and press lightly into a glass bowl filling the bottom third. Pour in enough of the chilled rhubarb juice to soak the sponge thoroughly, spoon in the rhubarb and top with a layer of custard. If you wish, spoon on a dollop of cream and a sprinkle of nuts. Chill well before serving.

Gooseberry Fool

Like the name trifle, this was considered just another frivolous little dessert, thus the name.

Top and tail 2lb (900g) gooseberries and put in a pan with ½ pint (275ml) water. Take 4 heads of elderflower, break them up and tie in a piece of muslin or fine cloth made into a bag. Drop this in the pan with the gooseberries and simmer until the fruit is tender. Remove and discard the elderflowers. Rub the gooseberries through a sieve. You will need 1 pint (570ml) puree. If not, make it up with juice and sweeten to taste. Allow to cool.

far left: Plums for eating or cooking
left: Enjoy the rich flavour of your own strawberries, freshly picked

Make a thick custard. Heat ¼ pint (150ml) milk, then pour gradually over 3 egg yolks, 1 tablespoon sugar and a teaspoon arrowroot beaten together in a bowl. Strain back into the pan and heat gently until the mixture thickens, then allow to cool. Combine it with the cool puree.

Whip ¼ pint (150ml) double cream and fold into the fruit custard, leaving it slightly marbled. Serve in individual glasses or bowls with sponge fingers.

Junket

Sterilise a large saucepan by pouring in a kettle of boiling water. Pour this out then add 2 litres fresh milk and a pinch of salt. Heat gently to blood temperature, as warm milk sours quicker and the curd will taste less bitter.

Remove from the heat and add 4 teaspoons rennet. Stir well, then leave for 15-20 minutes until the curds and whey have separated and it has 'jellied'. Pour off as much whey as possible then scoop out the curds into a double piece of muslin or a jelly bag and hang up for about 3 hours to allow it to drip over a basin. Remove and add a few drops of vanilla essence and a spoonful of sugar.

Serve with a sliced banana and a trickle of runny honey, strawberries, raspberries, stewed rhubarb or any other fruit in season as an alternative to cream.

Fruit Jelly Dessert

Put 1lb (450g) raspberries and ½lb (225g) redcurrants into a saucepan with ¾lb (350g) granulated sugar and ½ pint (27584ml) water. Stir over gentle heat until sugar has dissolved, then rub through a sieve. Measure the syrup and allow ¾oz (15g) of gelatine to each pint of puree. Soak gelatine in a little water using 3 tablespoons of water for every ¾ oz (15g) gelatine. Add this to the syrup and stir well. Pour into a wet mould until set.

Bramble Mousse

Put 1lb (450g) blackberries in a pan with 1oz (25g) caster sugar and stew gently until soft and pulpy. Rub them through a sieve and leave to cool.

Whisk 3 eggs with 2oz (50g) caster sugar together in a basin over a pan of hot water until thick. Soak ½oz (10g) gelatine in the juice of 1 lemon and 2 tablespoons water and dissolve over gentle heat. Lightly whip ¼ pint (150ml) double cream. Combine the egg/sugar mix with the gelatine mix and half the fruit puree, folding them in lightly, stirring the mixture over cold water until it begins to thicken. Pour into a glass bowl and chill. Just before serving, spoon the remaining puree mixture over the mousse and decorate with cream piped in a lattice design.

Fruit Cream

When there is a lot of rain about fruit is limited and less than perfect but it's ideal to make into fruit cream.

To make a raspberry cream, rub ½lb (225g) raspberries through a sieve - or liquidize. Save a few of the best for decoration. Gradually add 4 tablespoons sifted icing sugar. Lightly whip ½ pint (275ml) double cream and combine this with the fruit puree. Chill.

Fruit cream can be served in a dish, a meringue nest or a brandy-snap basket

Serve in individual dishes – with sponge fingers or ratafia biscuits (button sized macaroons, strongly flavoured with almonds). Scoop over strawberries or other fruit. Spoon into brandy snap baskets or meringues. For presentation, dust with icing sugar and decorate with a raspberry and mint leaves.

Fruit Compote

Compote is a term given to fruit cooked in a syrup. It is stewed fruit to most people, but to make a true compote first make a syrup. Average proportions would be 4 rounded tablespoons of granulated sugar to ½ pint (275ml) water per lb (450g) fruit. Instead of using ½ pint (275ml) water to make the syrup, you could use ¼ pint (150ml) water and ¼ pint (150ml) wine. Flavour the syrup with a strip of pared lemon rind, cinnamon stick or vanilla pod. Heat until the sugar has dissolved, then boil rapidly for 2 minutes before adding the fruit.

Apricots, plums and pears are ideal for compote. Cut in half and de-stone apricots and plums; peel pears and apricots. Place the prepared fruit, rounded side down in a pan of syrup and bring very slowly to the boil, allowing it to boil up and cover the fruit. Reduce the heat and simmer gently until fruit is tender. Pears will need 15 minutes to ensure they are soaked with syrup to prevent them discolouring when cool.

Serve with ice cream, whipped cream or fruit cream sprinkled with praline (see toffee recipes) or chocolate caraque.

Peach Melba

Poach four peaches cut in half, peeled and de-stoned, using the above method. Allow to cool in the syrup, drain and chill. Just before serving, place a scoop of vanilla ice-cream in each individual coupe glass, arrange two peach halves over it, coat with a tablespoon of the syrup and a tablespoon fruit puree. Top with a rosette of cream.

Toppings

Dame Nellie Melbourne had the famous dessert Peach Melba named after her, so why not personalize your own creation with the addition of something extra. Here are a selection of creams, sauces and syrups to spoon over pies and fruit to vary your dishes.

Fruit Puree

Rub 8oz (225g) raspberries through a sieve, liquidize or crush with a rolling pin or potato masher. Add 4 tablespoons of sifted icing sugar and a squeeze of lemon juice. Use as a sauce over a pudding, fruit or ice cream. Make into ice cream or mousses, or freeze for later use.

Mock Cream

Mix 3 teaspoons cornflour to a smooth paste with 2 fluid oz (70ml) water. Add 10 fluid oz (275ml) boiling milk and cook for two or three minutes to make a creamy sauce. Leave to cool. Cream 3oz (75g) margarine with 2 tablespoons sugar. Add a little vanilla essence, then beat into the cold sauce. Refrigerate until needed. Ideal on fruit and pies.

Hard Sauce

Cream 1 cup of softened butter with ½ cup icing sugar, caster or brown sugar until fluffy. Gradually add 2 tablespoons of either rum, brandy, fruit puree or coffee essence, then beat in another tablespoon of sugar. Refrigerate until needed. Perfect to serve with steamed puddings. Brandy Butter and Rum Butter are the hard sauces that are traditional toppings for mincepies and Christmas puddings

Yummy Chocolate Sauce

In a pan, combine 1 cup of cocoa, 1 generous tablespoon golden syrup, 1 tablespoon sugar, ½ cup water, 1 tablespoon butter and 1 tablespoon rum. Stir over a low heat until ingredients are melted then boil for 2 minutes.

Chocolate Sauce

Melt 4oz (113.4g) chocolate, and gradually stir in a small can of evaporated milk. Beat well and serve poured over profiteroles (page 43), fruit, ice cream, pancakes or pie.

Easy Toffee Sauce

Melt some toffee (see recipe) in a pan with a little milk, then pour it over fruit, ice cream, pancakes or pie.

Chocolate Caraque

Break 3oz (75g) plain block chocolate onto a plate over a pan of steadily boiling water. As the chocolate melts, work with a knife until smooth, then spread this thinly over a marble slab or laminated surface and leave until nearly set. Then, using a long, sharp knife held almost upright, shave the chocolate off the slab slantwise, using a slight sawing motion. The chocolate will form long rolls or flakes which can be used to top your desserts. They will keep for a while in an airtight tin.

Rubble

Use biscuit crumbs to sprinkle a golden rubble on top of fruit, ice cream, pancakes or pie.

Lip Smacking Syrup

Take 6-8 sugar lumps and rub them over the peel of an orange until they are soaked with oil zest. Squeeze the juice from the orange, pour over the crushed sugar lumps and add a small glass of brandy (2 fl oz). Stir well then pour the syrup over strawberries or the fruit of your choice. Chill for 2-3 hours before serving.

Chantilly Cream

Whisk ½ pint (275ml) double cream and when it begins to thicken add 3-4 teaspoons of vanilla sugar, or 2-3 drops of vanilla essence and 3-4 teaspoons of caster sugar.

Vanilla sugar is delicately flavoured fine caster sugar stored in a jar with 1-2 vanilla pods, the seed pods of a climbing orchid, native to the tropical rain-forests of central America. It reached Britain in the 17th century and became an established flavour for many desserts.

Ice Puddings

Keeping foods fresh and cool was always a major problem. Larger houses had cool cellars and pantries where there was usually a thick stone or marble slab. It wasn't until the 1920s and 30s that wealthy households began to acquire refrigerators.

Prior to this, the wealthy had ice-houses or ice-wells, brick or stone-lined pits, wholly or partly subterranean and often built into a bank of earth for insulation. When winter weather meant ice and snow, it was common for lakes and rivers to freeze over and this layer of ice was cut and carried to the ice-houses of the gentry where it was laid in alternate layers with straw, sometimes around joints of meat. Ice was also stored in this way for transfer to indoor pantries to keep fresh food chilled.

The Ice House at Chatsworth was used until the 1930s. Probably the last ice-house to be built locally was in 1890 and added to the new Darley Dale Hydropathic Establishment, later St Elphin's School and now private housing. An extremely well-preserved example lies in the former grounds of Middleton Hall near Youlgreave. Built against a grassy bank this ice-house consists of a short, flagged passage which ends at the rim of a twenty feet deep stone pit.

left: Everyone likes an ice cream
below: Frederick's 1953 ice-cream van

Frozen confections were described as 'iced puddings' and were very fashionable. They made known the wealth of the host. At least one elaborate, moulded iced pudding was always served at a formal dinner or banquet, and during a long menu, sorbets or water ices were served between the entrée and the roast to refresh the palate.

For most people their first taste of iced food came from the ice-cream man who toured the streets selling golden ice-cream. The Frederick family are Italian artisan ice-cream makers whose ancestor Angelo Manfredi started delighting British taste buds back in the 1890s with an ice cream that is still made to this day using virtually the same techniques and known as the Original 1898 blend. *'Ecco un poco'*, is what Angelo called as he rang his bell while pushing his ice-cream barrow round the Derbyshire streets. Victorian children were allowed a small taste of this rare delight, the first frozen product ever to be tasted by the working classes. The taste caught on and delighted children announced his arrival with – *'Here comes the Hokey-Pockey man'*.

Remembering her childhood in Morton in the 1920s, a 92 year old lady recalled an ice-cream man called Dicky French. On Friday night and Saturday afternoon, he went round with his pony and trap selling ice-cream from a churn. They had what were called penny licks, a small scoop of ice-cream served in a special pressed glass called a hokey-pokey cup, that gave a deceptive impression of the amount. This was licked out and handed back for the next customer. They were made illegal for public health reasons in 1926.

Tea Time Treats

Fifty years ago people referred to tea by the brand name of *Brooke Bond* or *Typhoo*. There was no mention of Darjeeling, Earl Grey or Lapsang Souchong. Now there are vast numbers of specialist teas and added to these are the herb and fruit infusions that are also referred to as teas. But tea is more than just a drink in England; the British make a meal of tea.

When tea becomes more than a warming, stimulating liquid and takes up its role as a meal, the drink can be accompanied by almost anything. Afternoon tea becomes tea at its most ceremonious and is usually taken at four o'clock. It's a light meal and a typical spread would included dainty, crustless sandwiches, fancy cakes, and scones with jam and cream. The adults who take afternoon tea eat dinner later, but for those who eat the more

Afternoon tea becomes tea at its most ceremonious

substantial high tea, which is usually served between six and seven, this combines the two meals into one. In some places it's called supper. A traditional Derbyshire high-tea would have ham, tongue, pork pie, sausage rolls, crusty bread, cheeses, crumpets, tea-cake, seed cake, carrot cake, fruit cake and all the other cakes for which Britain is deservedly famous.

Cakes were originally a dough with currants and spices. When the farm wives made batches of bread they reserved a piece to which fruit and spices were added, so the words bun, cake and bread became confused because of the similarity of the ingredients. By the end of the 18th century, bread was the basic nourishing commodity, the name bun was given to a sweet dough, and cake was a sweet batter leavened by an agent other than yeast. Of course there is always an exception to every rule – so we get currant bread and buns that are round and hold savoury fillings like beefburgers.

Flour is the basis of various cake mixtures to which rising agents are added to make them light, palatable and more easily digested. Before the introduction of chemical raising agents, yeast was bought from the brewer as liquid barm, or if yeast was not used, air was introduced into the mixture by folding in beaten eggs giving us such delights as the Invalid Sponge Cake that requires the use of eggs as a rising agent to make a fat-less sponge.

Some Victorian recipes instructed the cook to add a rising agent called volatile salts which is ammonium bicarbonate. The Wirksworth Wakes Cake recipe uses carbonate of ammonia. It made the cakes light and crisp, but the strong ammonia flavour had to be removed during cooking and the kitchen reeked of ammonia.

Once bicarbonate of soda, cream of tartar or acid phosphate were being used as a raising agent, this simplified cake making. Then Alexander MacDougal added rising agents to the flour during manufacture and thus invented self-raising flour. This simplified cake making to such an extent that a new boom in recipes. What few people know is that Alexander MacDougal

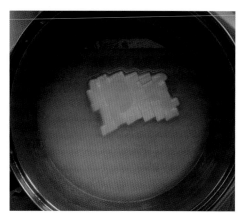

married Jane Shimwell, the youngest daughter of the landlord of the Bull's Head in the Derbyshire village of Youlgreave. If you prefer to use plain flour and a separate raising agent, to every 8oz (226.8g) plain flour, add 1 teaspoon cream of tartar and ½ teaspoon bicarbonate of soda, or 2 teaspoons baking powder.

Victoria Sandwich

Showing loyalty to the crown and country, this tea time treat was named in honour of the Queen, and in order to make it easy for everyone to make without having to weigh and measure all the ingredients, it was rather cleverly calculated in 'egg weight'. In other words, having the equivalent weight of the eggs in the other ingredients. For a Victoria sandwich you will need the weight of 4 eggs in luxury margarine or butter, in caster sugar, and in self-raising flour. Cream the margarine and sugar until light and fluffy. Break the

eggs, beat and add gradually to the margarine/sugar mixture, adding flour at intervals. Mix thoroughly, adding a drop of milk if its too stiff. Grease two 8"-9" sandwich tins and divide the mixture between them. Bake in a pre-heated moderate oven for 20 minutes or until golden. Turn out and when cold sandwich together with jam and dust the top with sifted icing sugar.

Butterfly Buns

These are a childhood favourite, so if you want to use eggs as weights, you will need two. Alternatively, here are the conventional weights too. Cream together 4oz (110g) soft butter and 4oz (110g) sugar until light and fluffy. Gradually add 1 teaspoon vanilla essence and 2 beaten eggs, alternating this with 4oz (110g) self-raising flour. Spoon the mixture into paper cake cases and bake in a pre-heated, moderately hot oven for 10 minutes or until

top and middle left: To make Gran's Cold Tea Cake, put all the ingredients in a pan and heat until the butter has melted
far left: The finished Cold Tea Cake
left: The Victoria sponge ready for dusting with a sprinkle of icing sugar

risen and golden. When cool gouge out a disc of cake from the top and cut this into two to form wings. Mix a small amount of buttercream using equal amounts of icing sugar and butter, creamed together with a dash of milk and put a scoop in each cake hollow. Press the 'wings' into this.

Seed Cake

This old stand-by was always served at funerals and high teas in Derbyshire.

Sift together 10oz (275g) self-raising flour and a pinch salt. In another bowl, cream together 5oz (150g) butter and 5oz (150g) sugar until light and fluffy. Beat in 3 teaspoons caraway seeds and one egg. Fold in the flour mixture and when the mixture is smooth, beat in 3 tablespoons milk. Pour the mixture into a greased cake tin, and bake in a pre-heated, moderate oven for 45 minutes.

top: To make butterfly buns, place paper cases in a patty pan and spoon in the mixture
middle and left: Bake until golden brown. Slice off the tops making a slight cavity, and pile in the butter icing. Cut the tops into two and set them in the butter icing so that they stick up like pairs of wings

Overnight Cake

Rub 8oz (225g) butter into 1lb (450g) flour. Add a pinch of salt, 8oz (225g) currants, 8oz (225g) sugar, 8oz (225g) raisins and ½ teaspoon nutmeg or spices. Mix 2 small teaspoons bicarbonate of soda with 2 teacups warm milk. Pour into dry ingredients and mix well. Pour into two greased bread tins and leave overnight. Bake 1½-2 hours in slow oven next day.

Invalid Sponge Cake

Beat 4 egg yolks with ¾ cup sugar. Beat egg whites and combine with another ¾ cup sugar. Beat well together, then lightly fold in 2 cups well-sifted flour, 2 tablespoons lemon juice and ½ cup cold water. Pour into a cake tin and bake in a moderate oven for 20-25 minutes or until the cake leaves the sides of the cake tin.

Nuttegs

Cream 4oz (110g) margarine with 4oz (110g) sugar. Add a well beaten egg, 1 cup of coconut, 4oz (110g) coarsely chopped walnuts and 3 cups of crisp cornflakes. Spoon the mixture into paper cake cases and bake in a pre-heated, slow oven for 20 minutes. (Makes 20 cakes)

Flap Jack

Melt 4oz (110g) butter or margarine, add 4oz (110g) sugar, 4oz (110g) oats and 1oz (25g) fine oatmeal. Mix well then press into a greased cake tin and bake in a slow over for 1½ to 2 hours.

top: To make Nuttegs, cream the butter and sugar, then mix in the coconut, walnuts and cornflakes
middle and left: Spoon the filling into the paper cases, and bake until golden brown

Courting Cake

In the days when it was considered that the way to a man's heart was through his stomach, a girl had to impress her boyfriend with her culinary skills, so this courting cake was traditionally made by a single girl to show her prowess in the kitchen. It rather reminds me of those antique needlework samplers – it shows a bit of all sorts to prove that, even if you haven't mastered all the techniques, you've grasped the concept. If the intended found this cake to his liking, he'd pop the question before she tried it out on another suitor.

Line a pie dish with short crust pastry and cover the bottom with a layer of raspberry jam, then a layer of stewed apples. Cover this with a sponge made from 4oz (110g) butter or margarine creamed with 4oz (110g) sugar, 2 eggs, a few drops of almond essence and 8 oz (225g) self-raising flour. Bake in a moderate oven until the sponge is well risen and firm to the touch. Allow to cool then cover the top with a layer of buttercream using 4oz (110g) icing sugar and 4oz (110g) butter, creamed together with a dash of milk.

For those who haven't got the time but still want to impress with their cooking, here is a fast cake – in fact it's so fast, it's called Lightning Cake.

Lightning Cake

Mix 1¾ cups self-raising flour, ½ teaspoon salt and 1 cup sugar. Add ¾ cup milk, ½ cup melted butter and 1 egg. Mix well then bake in a medium oven for an hour. Remove from the oven, but before removing the cake from the tin make the topping by mixing together 3 tablespoons butter/ margarine,

below: To make lightening cake, give all the ingredients a quick whisk, pour into a cake tin and cook for an hour.
bottom left: Before removing the cake from the tin, spread on the topping and brown under the grill
bottom right: Place on a cake stand and enjoy

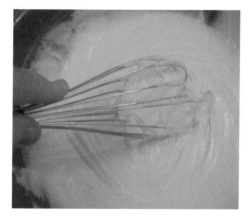

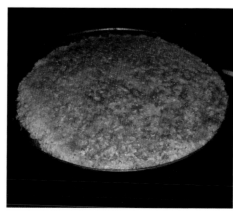

2 tablespoons cream or top of the milk, 5 tablespoons brown sugar and ½ cup desiccated coconut. Spread on top of the warm cake and brown under the grill. Remove the cake tin, place on a wire rack and allow to cool.

Lightning Cake leads on to Thor cakes named after the God of Thunder. These cakes have their origin in mythology as it was thought that they were eaten in honour of the feast day of the Scandinavian god Thor. Thor cakes are a similar mixture to parkin, but are formed into biscuits rather than a slab of cake. Both Thor cakes and parkin would traditionally be made and eaten on bonfire night and during the country wakes weeks. Recipes differ and so did their appearances. Most would appear to be like biscuits, but according to Allison Uttley, their Cromford version was rolled out to 2 inches (5cm) before cooking. It was served as a mid-morning snack sliced and spread with butter

Thor Cakes

Mix together 1 teaspoon ginger, 1lb (450g) flour, 1lb (450g) oatmeal, 1lb (450g) sugar, 2 teaspoon baking powder, 1 teaspoon salt and 1 teaspoon coriander or caraway seeds. Rub in 12oz (350g) butter, then add 1lb (450g) warm golden syrup. Knead a little, then roll out fairly thinly on a floured board and cut into rounds. Bake in a moderate oven for about ten minutes.

Castleton and Carsington, although some twenty five miles apart share the same recipe for Thor cakes, but Bradwell Thor Cake is slightly different as it uses half the quantities except butter and adds coriander seed.

Castleton and Carsington Thor Cakes

Rub ¾lb (350g) butter into 1lb (450g) self-raising flour, then add ½ teaspoon salt, 1lb (450g) demerara sugar, 1lb (450g) fine oatmeal, 1 teaspoon ginger and 1oz (25g) candied peel (optional). Mix well. Warm 1lb (450g) treacle (golden syrup) and pour into the dry ingredients. Knead well, then roll out to approximately ½ inch (1cm) thick. Cut out 25 rounds, place them on a baking tray in a moderate oven.

Bradwell Thor Cakes

Rub ¾lb (350g) butter into ½lb (225g) self-raising flour, then add ½ teaspoon salt, ½lb (225g) sugar, ½lb (225g) fine oatmeal, ½ teaspoon ginger, ½ teaspoon coriander seeds and 1oz (25g) candied peel (optional). Mix well. Warm ½lb (225g) treacle (golden syrup) and pour into the dry ingredients. Knead well, then roll out to approximately ½ inch (1cm) thick. Cut out 25 rounds, place them on a baking tray in a moderate oven.

right: Mix all the ingredients for Thor cakes, then knead the biscuit mix until smooth. Roll out and cut into rounds, Bake and serve when cold

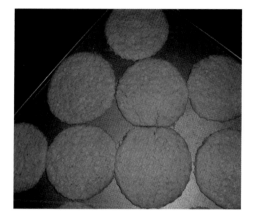

Samhain and Cakin Neet

The festival of Samhain on November 1st signalled the end of summer and the beginning of winter. It was a time when the veil between the world of the living and the dead was temporarily drawn away, allowing mortal men to communicate with the inhabitants of the otherworld. Samhain was a night when witches, warlocks, goblins and other evil spirits were free to wander the world of man.

The Christian festivals of All Saints and All Souls - known in the Medieval times as All Hallows was designed to coincide with and suppress the pagan festival of Samhain, but in practice, the celebration came to be held on the eve of All Hallows - which became known as Hallowe'en. The making of Thor cakes and Parkin can be traced back to pagan times as they were originally made to welcome the dead back to earth. In Bradfield, these cakes were baked and taken to the churchyard at night where they were left for the dead.

In the hilly Peak land around the villages of Stannington and Bradfield the night of Samhain is known as Cakin Neet. Children don masks before setting out to tour the houses of the district where they would knock on the doors and call *'copper, copper, cake, cake'*. The house-holders would try to guess the identity of the children, and if they failed, they had to pay in coppers, a slang name for pennies. If they guessed correctly, they handed out pieces of parkin or thor cakes. This is a Derbyshire tradition that dates back many hundreds of years before the commercial revival of Halloween imported from America.

Communal bonfires usually marked the night of October 31st. On top was hoisted an effigy, a scape-goat figure that absorbed all the evil and negative vibes of the community. When these bonfires were moved to November 5th, this figure evolved into Guy Fawkes. Traditionally bonfire food was a large potato baked in the ashes of the fire, and eaten with a sprinkle of salt. As the fire died down a tin of parkin would be passed round the adults. Each would take a piece as if they were drawing lots, and the one who chose a burnt, blackened piece would then have to leap over the dying embers of the fire to the accompaniment of a lot of goading and taunting.

Hallowe'en Parkin

Put 2lb (900g) fine oatmeal in a bowl and rub in ½lb (225g) butter or lard. Add 1lb (450g) sugar, a teaspoon ginger, 1lb (450g) good treacle, and 1 teaspoon bicarbonate of soda dissolved in one teaspoon of milk. Spoon into a well greased roasting tin and bake in a pre-heated moderate oven for one hour or until risen, then turn heat to slow for a further hour.

Derbyshire Parkin

Mix together 1lb (450g) self-raising flour, 1lb (450g) fine oatmeal, ½ teaspoon salt and 1 teaspoon ginger. Melt 1lb (450g) demerara sugar, 1lb (450g) golden syrup and ¾lb (350g) butter. Pour this into the dry ingredients and mix to a stiff batter with a good splash of milk. Spoon into a well-greased roasting tin in a slow – moderate oven for approximately 45 minutes.

Ashbourne Gingerbread

The Gingerbread Shop in the heart of Ashbourne is a unique example of a late 15th century timber framed building similar to most of the houses and shops that originally stood in the centre of this delightful south Derbyshire town. In the 17th century, the building became the Roebuck Inn until the Napoleonic Wars when it became a bakery.

During that period, French prisoners of war were held in Ashbourne. In 1804, there were more than 200 French officers held here, among them were three of Napoleon's Generals, Boyer, Pajeau and Roussambeau who, with their retinues, reputedly spent £30,000 annually in the town. It is said that the original gingerbread recipe came from these soldiers who missed the taste of the biscuit they knew which comes from the Dijon region of France.

The Ashbourne Gingerbread Shop has been in continuous use as a bakery since 1805 and has been making gingerbread all this time, but unlike the Bakewell pudding there doesn't appear to be one closely guarded secret recipe. Until the 19th century, gingerbread was boiled rather than baked, and the basic ingredients were breadcrumbs, ginger, liquorice, aniseed and cinnamon. The use of breadcrumbs would solve the origin of the name gingerbread. Later variations added butter, sugar, treacle, beer, ground almonds, oatmeal, honey, cinnamon, caraway seeds, mixed spice and coriander. The mixture would then be pressed into decorative or scenic wooden moulds made from straight grained fruit woods like pear or apple that would give a raised design. Rather like the variety in the ingredients, the variety in moulds

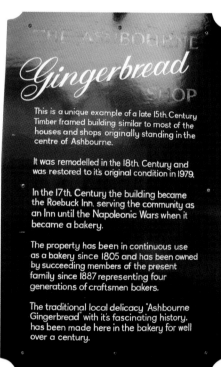

This is a unique example of a late 15th. Century Timber framed building similar to most of the houses and shops originally standing in the centre of Ashbourne.

It was remodelled in the 18th. Century and was restored to it's original condition in 1979.

In the 17th. Century the building became the Roebuck Inn. serving the community as an Inn until the Napoleonic Wars when it became a bakery.

The property has been in continuous use as a bakery since 1805 and has been owned by succeeding members of the present family since 1887 representing four generations of craftsmen bakers.

The traditional local delicacy "Ashbourne Gingerbread" with it's fascinating history. has been made here in the bakery for well over a century.

was immense and in 1825, this even prompted J Crane to write a little ode which he included in his book *Poems to a Bard*.

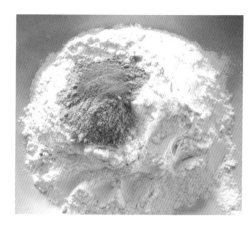

> *The bakers to increase their trade*
> *Made alphabets of gingerbread*
> *That folks might swallow what*
> * they read*
> *All the letters were digested*
> *Hateful, ignorance, detested*

Ashbourne Gingerbread Men

Sift 1lb (450g) plain flour, 1 dessertspoon bicarbonate of soda, 1 dessertspoon ground ginger, ½ teaspoon ground cinnamon and ½ teaspoon salt into a mixing bowl. Stir in 8oz (225g) soft brown sugar. Place 4oz (110g) butter and 1 teacup of golden syrup in a bowl and heat until the butter has melted. Stir this into the dry ingredients adding a splash of milk if the mix is too stiff.

left: The Ashbourne Gingerbread Shop with its sign
right: Spoon the dry ingredients into a bowl. Mix in melted butter and syrup. Work until the mixture is a smooth ball Place paper patterns on the rolled out dough – Cut round the pattern with a sharp knife and decorate with smarties. Bake then pipe details on the shapes to finish off

Work the mixture with a knife, then knead with your hand until it is a smooth ball with a surface sheen. It will feel pleasantly warm so place in the 'fridge for half an hour.

Meanwhile make a paper pattern. To get both sides even fold the paper in half and mark half the body on one side. Cut and open out to get the pattern.

Roll out the gingerbread mixture to about ½ inch (1cm) thick. To get it even, place two table mats on the surface, far enough apart to be able to roll the mixture between, but close enough to have either end of the rolling pin rolling on the mats. Lay the pattern in place, and cut round with a sharp knife. Remove the paper pattern and lift the cut out dough carefully onto a baking tray lined with greaseproof paper. A small piece of glace cherry for the mouth and currants or smarties for the eyes and buttons are optional. Bake in a pre-heated moderate oven for 20 minutes or until golden. Mix 1 tablespoon icing sugar and a small amount of water to make a white icing thin enough to pipe, and place in an icing bag with a fine nozzle. When the gingerbread men are cold, outline eyes, nose, mouth, shoes, shirt cuffs and collar as you like.

Ashbourne Gingerbread Biscuits

Cream 8oz (225g) butter/margarine with 5oz (150g) sugar. Stir in 10oz (275g) plain flour, 2 teaspoons ground ginger, twist of salt and teaspoon finely grated lemon peel. Knead into a smooth dough, then form into a long roll like a fat sausage. Cut into slices about 1inch thick. Put onto a greased baking tin and press down to thin. Bake for 20 minutes in a moderate oven.

Ginger Nuts

The commercial ginger nut is on the hard side of crisp, but what it loses in tenderness it makes up for in dunkability. If dipped for just the right amount of time, it will soften to the perfect degree without disintegrating and landing back in your cup to form a sludgy deposit.

Sift together 4oz (110g) self-raising flour, ½ level teaspoon bicarbonate of soda, 1-2 teaspoon ground ginger, 1 teaspoon ground cinnamon and 2oz (50g) sugar. Melt 2oz (50g) margarine/butter and stir in 3 tablespoons golden syrup. Add to the dry ingredients and mix to a fairly stiff consistency. Divide into two then two again and divide each piece into 6 until you have 24 equal pieces. Roll each piece into a ball.

Space them well on a couple of greased baking sheets, flatten and bake in a pre-heated moderate oven for 10-15 minutes.

Rich Gingerbread Biscuits

This is more chic than the common ginger nut but with the same essential network of surface cracks. The more upmarket the biscuit the wider the cracks.

Sift together 4oz (110g) plain flour, twist of salt, 1 teaspoon baking powder, 1 teaspoon bicarbonate of soda, 1 teaspoon ground ginger, ½ teaspoon ground mixed spice. Rub in 2oz (50g) margarine/butter. Add 2oz (50g) sugar, 3 tablespoons warm golden syrup and one teaspoon brandy (optional). Mix to a fairly stiff consistency. Divide into two, then two again, and divide each piece into 6, until you have 24 equal pieces. Roll each piece into a ball. Space them well on a couple of greased baking sheets, flatten and bake in a pre-heated moderately hot oven for 6-8 minutes.

Soft Gingerbread

Cream 4oz (110g) margarine/ butter and 3oz (75g) sugar together, add 1 well beaten egg, 8oz (225g) flour, 1½ teaspoons ginger and 3oz (75g) golden syrup. Dissolve 1 teaspoon bicarbonate of soda in one third of a teacup of boiling water and stir into other ingredients. Put in a flat roasting tin and bake in a pre-heated moderate oven for 30 minutes. When cool, cut into squares.

Brandy Snaps

The same gingery biscuit taste but this is a crisp biscuit formed into a cylinder after baking but while still pliable.

Melt 2oz (50g) butter/margarine, 2 oz (50g) sugar, and 2oz (50g) golden syrup in a pan. Remove from the heat and stir in 2oz (50g) plain flour, 1 teaspoon ground ginger, 1 teaspoon brandy (optional). Grease a number of baking trays. Drop small spoonfuls of the mixture onto the trays allowing room for them to expand. Bake in a pre-heated, moderate oven for 7-10 minutes. In the meantime, grease the handles of several wooden spoons. When the mixture is bubbly and golden, remove from the oven, allow to cool for a minute, loosen with a palette knife then while each biscuit is still pliable, roll round a spoon handle. As they set they will hold their tubular shape when you slip them off the handles. If they cool too much while still on the tray, they will be too hard and brittle to roll, so pop them back in the oven until they have softened, then roll. When they are cool, the ends can be dipped in chocolate and they can be filled with whipped cream for immediate use or store them in an airtight tin

Brandy Snap Baskets

Use the brandy snap recipe and proceed until the mixture is bubbly and golden. Remove from the oven, allow to cool for a minute, loosen with a palette knife and instead of rolling them round spoon handles, have several small, inverted moulds ready greased. If you have no moulds, use small jam jars or cups, although the handles tend to get in the way. Simply drape the pliable biscuits over each mould and as they set they will hold their shape. If they cool too much while still on the tray, they will be too hard and brittle to drape, so pop them back in the oven until they have softened, then drape. Remove when cold and fill the basket shape with fruit or any cream based dessert. The unfilled baskets will store well in an airtight tin.

The Wakes

The original meaning of a wake is a solemn watch or ceremonial vigil spent in the church on the eve of the saint day to whom the church was dedicated. The night spent in prayer was followed by a day's celebration. It became the annual holy day (holiday) of the district, and as early as 1203 Hartington was granted a three day fair at the Feast of St Giles. In 1250, Tideswell gained the right to hold a two day fair at the Decollation of St John the Baptist and over the centuries the custom became very wide-spread.

In the middle ages, a travelling fair visited each village to coincide with their wake and the fairground people sold sugar and spices. These were commodities that couldn't generally be bought locally, and there was a good sale amongst the villagers who customarily used honey for sweetening. The fairground people also brought sideshows that would be set up on the village green. Streets and houses were decorated, schools and mills closed for a holiday. Many White Peak villages incorporated well-dressing into the festivities.

By Georgian times entertainment included bull, bear and badger baiting, organised cock-fights and dog-fights, bare knuckle boxing matches and freak shows. Then arrived the great steam engines with their loads of gaily decorated round-abouts and the living caravans towed behind. The Wake had taken on a different meaning and had become plural – wakes. It was now more secular that spiritual.

There were chip and pea stalls, and pie and pea stalls; the peas were always mushy. The Wakes had gingerbread stalls with London curl, brandy snaps, gingerbread men and ginger nuts. There were always coconuts at wakes, a rarity that people didn't normally see at any other time of the year. If you knocked the coconut off its stand, or someone did it for you, the coconut was your prize.

The holiday atmosphere attracted large crowds and the spirit of old English hospitality was conspicuous among the villagers. In one guide book from the 1950s it actually said *'villagers hastened to put on the kettle for the curious and welcome visitors who attended the wakes'*. They would also be offered a piece of Wakes Cake and each village had its own recipe.

Ashbourne Wakes Cakes

Cream 2 cups of butter, 2 cups of sugar and 4 teaspoons ground ginger. Add 1 beaten egg, finely shredded lemon peel and 4 cups flour. Mix to form a firm dough. Roll out very thin on a floured surface. Cut into rounds. Press in a few currants and bake in a moderate oven until crisp and lightly browned.

Winster Wakes Cake

Rub 8oz (225g) plain flour and 6oz (175g) butter together. Add 6oz (175g) sugar and 1oz (25g) currants. Mix to a firm dough with a beaten egg. Knead, then roll out to the size of a saucer and bake in a moderate oven until pale golden brown

Melbourne Wakes Cakes

Sieve 1¾lbs (800g) flour with 2 teaspoons baking powder, rub in 1lb (450g) butter, add ½lb (225g) sugar and ¼ lb (110g) currants. Mix with 2 eggs and a little milk/cream. Roll out thinly, cut like biscuits and bake in a moderate oven until light brown. Sprinkle with sugar and store in a tin.

Langley Wakes Cake

Sieve 1lb (450g) flour with 2 teaspoons baking powder, rub in ½lb (225g) butter, add 6oz (175g) sugar, ½oz (10g) caraway seeds and ¼lb (110g) currants. Mix with 2 eggs and milk/cream. Roll out thinly, cut like biscuits and bake in a moderate oven until light brown. Sprinkle with sugar and serve.

Wirksworth Wakes Cake

Cream 1lb (450g) butter and 1lb (450g) sugar and add 1 teaspoon carbonate of ammonia (substitute baking powder for the carbonate of ammonia). Stir in 1½lb (675g) flour, twist of salt, ¼lb (110g) currants, ½oz (10g) caraway seed and milk/cream to mix. Roll out thinly and cut into rounds. Bake in a moderate oven until pale brown.

Sugar Cakes
another fairground favourite

Rub 10 oz (275g) butter/margarine into 1lb (450g) plain flour until it resembles fine breadcrumbs. Stir in 9oz (250g) sugar and finely grated peel of 1 lemon. Bind to a manageable dough with 1 large beaten egg. Divide the mixture into four and work each piece in turn. Divide the ¼ into 8 equal parts and on a lightly floured surface, roll each piece into a 12" (30cm) rope. Cut each rope in three 4" (10cm) lengths. Take two lengths and twist them together. Fold one end round to form a hook and place on a greased baking sheet in a pre-heated moderate oven for 10-15 minutes. Cool, then dredge with icing sugar before eating.

right: Edible art made from shortbread to hang on the Christmas tree

Shortbread

These golden, buttery, bite sized rounds are melt in the mouth perfection that you can enjoy all year round but as everyone gets nibbly at Christmas, why not create some edible art like Grandma used to bake to hang on the Christmas tree.

Like egg-nog and plum pudding, tree decorations made of biscuits were a Victorian tradition. You can occasionally still find old wooden gingerbread or butter moulds to give a raised design although these are not usually seasonal. Cutters are now made in plastic, but if you don't have a cutter use the floured rim of a drinking glass. Or why not create personalized, freehand designs from your own templates using seasonal shapes like bells, Christmas wreaths, Christmas trees and stars?

Beat together 7oz (200g) soft butter and 2oz (50g) sifted icing sugar until light and fluffy. Combine 4oz (110g) sifted self-raising flour, 5oz (150g) sifted plain flour and 1 tablespoon cornflour. Mix all ingredients and knead lightly to make a smooth dough. Wrap in cling film and chill for 30 minutes. If using a mould, sprinkle it liberally with flour then tap gently to release the excess. Take a knob of dough and press this into the mould. Cut off the excess with a sharp knife, remove the dough carefully, make a hole for hanging and place on a baking sheet. These biscuits will have a two dimensional effect and resemble mini tiles or wall plaques.

If using a template or a cutter, lightly flour a pastry board and roll out dough to ¼" (6mm) thick. Cut out the biscuit shapes and place on a baking tray. If you want to make a raised plaque by superimposing your own design, roll the remaining dough thinner and press the decoration firmly onto the biscuit. If you want to hang the biscuits, pierce with a meat skewer then place them on a baking sheet. Cook in a moderate oven for 15 minutes. Cool for one minute then transfer to a wire rack and decorate when cold.

To decorate, make a glaze icing with 2oz (50g) icing sugar and ½-1 tablespoon lemon juice or warm water to form a consistency that will coat the spoon. If you want to add more intricate details that can't be clearly defined in dough, make Royal icing. Place one egg white in a bowl and beat to a firm foam. Gradually add 6oz (175g) icing sugar and a splash of strained lemon juice to make a coating consistency and apply a thin coat to the biscuit. Leave to thoroughly dry, preferably overnight than use like a canvas and paint on your details with edible food dyes.

Lavender shortbread has the unusual addition of lavender flowers. Bake until slightly tinged and mark into squares before removing from the baking tray. Serve them for tea, keep them in an airtight tin or put them in a pretty box and give as a present

Allow to dry before threading the biscuits with a loop of fine red ribbon or decorative string to hang on your Christmas tree.

Derbyshire Lavender Shortbread

Lavender along with other edible flowers such as violets and roses were widely used in cookery in days gone by and this recipe smells and tastes delicious.

Pick 2 teaspoons fresh lavender flowers. Beat together 6oz (175g) softened unsalted butter and 3oz (75g) sugar until pale and fluffy. Sift in 9oz (250g) plain flour and 3oz (75g) corn flour. Add the lavender flower heads and mix well until the mixture resembles fine bread-crumbs. Spoon onto a well-greased baking tray. Level and press down to compact the mixture. Bake in a pre-heated slow oven for 20-25 minutes or until lightly coloured. Remove and sprinkle with caster sugar and while still on the baking tray, with a knife divide the still-soft biscuit into fingers. Leave to cool and harden then carefully cut through the knife marks and store in a tin.

right (top to bottom): Caudwell's Mill, flour stocks and sign

Digestive Biscuits

Mix 4oz (110g) wholemeal flour, 4oz (110g) medium oatmeal, 1 small teaspoon bicarbonate of soda, twist of salt and 1 tablespoon sugar. Rub in 2oz (50g) margarine. Add 1 beaten egg and a little milk if necessary. Roll out thinly, and use a cutter to make biscuits. Prick all over, place on greased tray and bake in pre-heated moderate oven for about 20 minutes. Allow to cool before removing from tray, but for extra indulgence, while still warm, grate chocolate over the biscuits. The heat of the biscuits will melt the chocolate and make it easy and economical to spread over the surface.

Caudwell's Ancient Flour Mill

Caudwell's Mill at Rowsley is Derbyshire's unique, grade II listed, historical flour mill, the only complete Victorian water turbine-powered roller mill in the country, power-driven by water from the River Wye.

A mill has stood on this site for at least 400 years. The present mill was built in 1874 by John Caudwell, using huge steel rollers rather than traditional millstones to grind the flour. It was run as a family business for over a century and now fully restored is one of the last of its kind operating in the country.

It uses the same process as the giant modern mills which provide most of the flour for our bread today, but at Caudwell's Mill, it is at a speed and on a scale that takes us back a hundred years. You are able to see four floors of fascinating, automatic machinery, most of which is still driven by belts, often leather, and pulleys from line shafts. Elevators and Archimedean screws abound. The mill is powered by two water turbines, the larger installed in 1914 to drive the flour mill and the smaller installed in 1898, for the provender mill and which, today, also generates the electricity used in the mill.

Caudwell's historic mill is open daily for flour sales with a choice of over 20 specialist flours.

Caudwell's Courgette Cake – grate the courgette – mix all the ingredients – finished cake

Caudwell's Courgette Cake

Mix together 8oz (225g) Caudwell's self-raising flour, ½ teaspoon baking powder, ½ teaspoon bicarbonate of soda, 5oz (150g) sugar, 3oz (75g) raisins, 9oz (250g) grated courgette – peel and all, 2 eggs and ¼ pint (150ml) olive oil. Pour into a cake tin and bake in a pre-heated moderate oven for 60-70 minutes.

Note: because of the moisture content, courgette cake does not keep for more than three days.

Chatsworth Boiled Fruit Cake

Place 8oz (225g) butter, 12oz (350g) sugar, 1½lb (675g) mixed fruit, 6oz (175g) cherries, 3 heaped teaspoons mixed spice, 2 level teaspoons bicarbonate of soda and ½ pint (275ml) water in a pan. Bring to the boil and simmer for one minute. Pour into a large bowl and allow to cool. Add 1lb (450g) Caudwell's strong white flour, twist of salt, 4 beaten eggs and 5 fl oz (150ml) brandy. Mix well then pour into a lined 10" square cake tin. Level the top and bake in centre of a pre-heated moderate oven for about 75 minutes.

Note: This is a large cake, but works well to divide the mixture and make two cakes.

Chatsworth Boiled Fruit Cake

Castleton Vicarage Cake

Put 1lb (450g) self-raising flour, ¾lb (350g) brown sugar, ½lb (225g) currants, ½lb (225g) sultanas and ¼lb (110g) candied peel into a bowl and mix. Make a well in the centre. Cut ¾lb (350g) butter into small pieces and drop these into the well. Bring ¼ pint (150ml) milk to the boil and pour over the butter, mix well. Put in a greased cake tin and bake in a preheated moderate oven for 2 hours.

Bolsover Cake

Beat together 12oz (350g) butter and 8oz (225g) sugar. Add 4 eggs and 1lb (450g) flour, then add ½ lb (225g) currants, ½lb (225g) raisins, 2oz (50g) candied peel and ½ wine glass sherry. Put in a greased cake tin and bake in a moderate oven for 2 hours or until a knitting needle comes out clean.

Jane Mosley's hand written recipe from 1690

To Make A Cake The Way Of The Royal Princes, The Lady Elizabeth, daughter to King Charles The First

Take halfe a peck of flower, halfe a pinte of rose water, a pint of ale, yeast, a pint of cream, boil it, a pound and a halfe of butter, six eggs, leaf out the white, four pound of currans, one half pound of sugar, one motmeg (nutmeg) and a little sal. Worke it very well and let it stand by the fire, then worke it againe and then make it up and let it stand an our and half in the oven; let not the oven be too hot.

right: Scones are the perfect accompaniment for afternoon tea
opposite page: Simnel Cake is traditionally served at Easter or Mothering Sunday

Scones

Sift 8oz (225g) self-raising flour, twist of salt and teaspoon baking powder together. Rub in 2oz (50g) margarine until the mixture resembles fine breadcrumbs. Make a well in the centre and stir in a tea cup milk or enough to make a soft dough. Turn onto a floured board and roll out lightly to about 1" (3cm) thick. Using a cutter or glass rim dipped in flour, cut 10-20 rounds, place on a baking sheet and bake in a pre-heated hot oven for 8-10 minutes. Cool, split and spread with butter and jam or a dollop of thick cream.

These plain scones are ideal with jam and cream, but fruit scones – with 2oz (50g) dried fruit added are perfect with butter.

The Singing Hinny

In some remote country areas you'll find the 'singing hinny', a scone type mixture made into one round cake cooked on a griddle where it sings and fizzes as it cooks – thus the name.

Ashover Rock Cakes

Sift 8oz (225g) self-raising flour, teaspoon baking powder, ½ teaspoon salt and ½ teaspoon mixed spice (optional). Rub in 4oz (110g) butter or margarine until the mixture resembles fine bread-

crumbs. Add grated peel of ½ a lemon (optional), 4oz (110g) demerara sugar, and 4oz (110g) mixed dried fruit. Make a well in the centre and stir in 1 beaten egg and 1 teaspoon milk to make a stiff, crumbly consistency. Using two forks, shape the mixture into 12 rough heaps. Place on a baking sheet and bake in a pre-heated moderately hot oven for 15-20 minutes.

Cromford Cakes

Mix 4 oz (110g) self-raising flour, 2oz (50g) sugar and ¼ pint (150ml) milk. Warm 1oz (25g) yeast with a little sugar and water and add to the dough. Add half a cup of mixed fruit. Shape the mixture into 12 rough heaps. Place on a baking sheet and bake in a pre-heated moderately hot oven for 15-20 minutes.

Fat Rascals

These were often made from left over pastry and eaten hot from the oven with butter spread between.

Rub 4oz (110g) soft butter into 8oz (225g) plain flour and a twist of salt. Add 2oz (50g) currants and 1oz (25g) brown sugar. Mix to a stiff dough with milk and roll out to about ½ inch (15mm) thick. Cut into rounds and sprinkle with caster sugar. Bake in a moderate oven for 15-20 minutes.

Simnel Cake

This seasonal cake is the traditional cake for Mothering Sunday and Easter. It is characteristically decorated with 11 marzipan balls on the top to represent the 12 apostles minus Judas. Mothering Sunday was the day when girls took their young men home to meet their mothers and a simnel cake was often given as a gift from the young man to his future mother-in-law.

I did hear that it got it's name because of an argument between Simon (Sim) and Nellie (Nell). who couldn't agree on the best way to make this cake so they made it in two halves separated by the marzipan layer, but don't quote me on that!

Cream 8oz (225g) soft butter and 8oz (225g) light brown sugar. Beat 3 eggs. Sift together 8oz (225g) plain flour, 2 level teaspoons baking powder, ½ teaspoon salt and 1 level teaspoon ground mixed spice. Add these to the butter mixture in turn

with the beaten eggs and juice of 1 lemon and 1 orange to form a well blended batter. Fold in the zest of 1 orange and 1 lemon, 8oz (225g) each of currants, sultanas and raisins, and 4oz (110g) chopped mixed candied peel (optional).

Put half the mixture into a greased cake tin and level the top. Take 6oz (175g) marzipan and roll out to a circle that fits the cake tin. Lay this on top of the cake mixture, then put the remaining mixture on top. Bake in the centre of a low oven for 2-2 ½ hours. Remove from the oven and leave to cool in the tin.

Overall you will need 1lb (450g) marzipan or, if you want to make your own, combine 12oz (350g) ground almonds, 8oz (225g) icing sugar, 3 beaten egg yokes and a squeeze of lemon juice to get a stiff paste. Divide it roughly into three. Use a third in the centre of the cake, make 11 balls from the second third. Roll out the remaining third into a circle the size of the cake.

Turn the cool cake out of the tin and brush the top with melted jam. Lay the circle of marzipan on top and place the 11 marzipan balls round the edge. Brush with a little beaten egg and put it under the grill for a few minutes to gild the marzipan a deep golden colour.

Aunty Hilda's Brandy fed Christmas Cake

Aunty Hilda's Brandy Fed Christmas Cake

Great Aunty Hilda, born at the end of the 19th century, gave me this recipe which she categorically declared never failed. It was my first attempt at a rich fruit cake and proved so successful it has remained a constant favourite.

Cream 8oz (225g) sugar, 8oz (225g) margarine/butter and 1 tablespoon treacle or golden syrup. Gradually add 4 well beaten eggs alternating with 10oz (275g) sifted flour – ½ self-raising, and ½ plain. Cut ¼ lb glace cherries and add with 1lb (450g) mixed fruit. Mix well, pour into a greased cake tin and bake in a slow oven for 1½-2 hours. Transfer to a wire rack to cool then pierce the top with a knitting needle and trickle 3 tablespoons brandy or other suitable spirit over the surface and watch it soak through the holes.

Store it in an airtight tin and add more brandy at intervals.

To make this into a real celebration cake, instead of the 1lb (450g) mixed fruit, cram it with a mixture of up to 2lb (900g) sun-soaked dried apricots, currants, sultanas, raisins and dates. Place these in a mixing bowl, pour over 3 tablespoons brandy and leave overnight to soak. To the flour add ¼ teaspoon grated nutmeg, ½ teaspoon ground mixed spice, ½ teaspoon salt, the grated zest of 1 orange, the grated zest of 1 lemon and 2oz (50g) chopped almonds. Cream the butter, sugar and treacle as above, combine all the ingredients, spoon into a 8 inch (20cm) greased cake tin and bake in a slow oven for 3½-4 hours. When using such long cooking times, tie a band of brown paper round the outside of the tin for extra protection, and cover the top of the cake with greaseproof paper with a 50p size hole cut in the centre.

When cold, douse the cake in brandy or whisky as above until you need to ice or eat it.

right: Before icing, cover the cake in a layer of marzipan. Fondant icing will drape like fabric. Dig out the old Christmas cake decorations or for a simple, effective Christmas cake that looks like a parcel, cut two lengths of ribbon to wrap over the cake in both directions, then finish off with a bow

The Icing On The Cake

When ready to ice the cake, make marzipan as in the recipe for Simnel Cake. Paint the cake with melted jam, lay a circle of marzipan on top and round the sides and leave for several days to dry out its oiliness.

Decide how you want to decorate the cake. Would you prefer a rough snow scene with a few plastic figures of Father Christmas, children sledging, chirpy robins and other seasonal subjects that are brought out and dusted off annually? If so, make royal icing with 1lb (450g) sifted icing sugar, 3 egg whites and a teaspoon glycerine. Combine and beat until the icing stands in peaks, then use a palette knife to smooth it over the marzipan on the cake. To roughen the snow, spike it by lifting the palette knife briskly, then add a sprig of holly or those little figures.

If you prefer something a little more sophisticated, make up fondant icing using 1¼ lb (560g) sifted icing sugar, 1½ egg whites (the other half is used as a glue to brush over the marzipan), and 140g bottle of liquid glucose. Mix well together, then knead in the same way that you would bread. Roll out with plenty of sifted icing sugar and spread over the egg-coated marzipan. Ease and smooth with a palette knife over the top and down the sides, then trim. This is now like a blank canvas. To make it look like a parcel, buy decorative ribbon and cut two lengths long enough to wrap across the cake in both directions, then make the remaining ribbon into a large bow and secure with large headed pins.

Alternatively, roll out the remaining fondant trimmings to decorate, and glue them in place with egg white.

Special Toffees and Sweets

Marzipan Fruits

Marzipan can be made into delicious little gourmet sweets, coloured and shaped like oranges, lemons, apples, bananas or dates. This is an ideal way to use up any excess marzipan after coating the Christmas cake.

Break off pieces of marzipan and colour each with a few drops of vegetable based food dye. Use the dye sparingly as it gives an intense colour that is difficult to remove. Knead each piece of marzipan thoroughly to obtain an even colour, then roll into the desired shape. For dates, use cocoa or gravy browning to get the brown colour. For fruit like peaches, apples, plums etc, use a paintbrush and one colour or a mixture of dyes to shade the fruit. Peaches and plums can be given their characteristic indentation marks with a teaspoon, and when dry, brushed with icing sugar for bloom. Roll strawberries and citrus fruit on a fine grater to give them their surface texture. Cloves make suitable stalks and calyxes for apples and pears but specialist confectionary shops sell plastic varieties.

Praline or Nut Brittle

This is not only a sweet in its own right, it can also be used to scatter on the tops of puddings or ice-cream. First roast the chopped nuts in a moderate oven for 6 minutes. Whatever weight of nuts, put the same weight of sugar into a pan and

To make praline or nut brittle, toast the nuts then chop them small, make a toffee syrup, throw in the nuts and pour into a grease tin to set. Use as a sweet, scatter over desserts or put in a tin and give as a present.

allow to melt slowly. When it turns a golden colour, toss in the nuts. Let the nuts caramelise, turn off the heat and pour the praline onto a greased baking tray to set.

Break into small pieces or to scatter on puddings use a liquidizer for a few seconds. Store until needed in a screw top jar.

Bonfire Toffee and Toffee Apples

These are a firm favourite and as much part of November 5th as bonfires and parkin. To make toffee it is advisable though not absolutely necessary to have a sugar thermometer which will indicate the exact setting times. Alternatively, drop half a teaspoon of the rapidly boiling toffee onto a saucer of cold water. When it sets solid, its ready. The same method is used for testing jams and jellies.

Dissolve 1lb (450g) sugar in just over ¼ pint (150ml) water, add 2oz (50g) butter, a pinch of cream of tartar and 1 dessertspoon vinegar. Boil steadily until setting temperature is reached, then pour into a greased shallow tin. Setting temperature for soft toffee is 270-310°F, hard toffee is 325°F.

To make Toffee Apples, wash and dry six eating apples and insert corn on the cob sticks or scewers through

the centre core. Make up the above toffee recipe, then when the toffee has reached 270°F, dip each apple in turn, turning to coat evenly, then stand on a greased tray to cool and harden.

top left: When the toffee is on the point of setting, dip your apple, twirl it in the toffee then leave to cool
middle left: When the toffee is on the point of setting pour it into a greased tin
left: Mark the toffee into squares before it is too hard
above: This is the toffee to hand round at Halloween and Bonfire night

Two Tone Toffee

Take two thick bottom pans. Put 1lb (450g) brown sugar, 4oz (110g) butter and 1 tablespoon of vinegar in each. Into one pan add 4 tablespoons of golden syrup. Into the other pan put 2 tablespoons of golden syrup and 2 tablespoons of treacle. Boil each pan for 20 minutes, then tip onto a cool surface and rapidly cool the mixtures until soft and pliable. Draw the mixture, roll it, plait or twist it together to form interesting shapes.

Barley Sugar Twists

This brittle, clear, amber coloured sweet was originally made by boiling sugar with barley extract, thus the name. It is frequently twisted into sticks that have given the name barley-sugar twist to similar shapes made in wood and stone.

Put 1lb (450g) sugar and ½ pint (275ml) water into a pan. When the sugar has melted, add a beaten egg white and a dash of lemon juice or essence. Stir well and when boiling remove scum and boil until clear. Strain through muslin and boil again. Test. It should be quite brittle and snap easily. Pour onto a flat dish or slab and cut into strips. Dip the hands in cold water and roll and twist the sticks. When cold, dust a little sifted sugar over.

Coconut Ice

Put 2lb (900g) sugar and ¾ pint (425ml) water in a pan and let it boil for about 10 minutes without colouring. Take it off the stove and stir in 1lb (450g) desiccated coconut. Pour into a tin and cut into squares before it cools.

Chocolate Fudge

Boil together 2 cups of sugar, 1 cup milk, a bar of chocolate and a lump of butter the size of an egg, for about 10 minutes or until it will make a soft ball in cold water. Take off the heat, stir and pour into a greased tin. Mark into squares when cold.

Nougat

Combine ¾ lb (350g) caster sugar, 5 fluid ounce (150ml) water, stirring all the time until the sugar has dissolved. Add 4oz (110g) liquid glucose and 1oz (25g) liquid honey. Increase heat and boil without stirring until it reaches 275ºF. Meanwhile whisk I large egg white with a pinch of cream of tartar. Gradually pour this into the hot syrup whisking all the time.

To make coconut ice, boil the syrup without allowing it to colour then stir in the coconut. Press into a shallow tin, mark into squares and allow to set

Continue whisking until the mixture begins to thicken, then quickly stir in 2oz (50g) chopped pieces of glace cherries, 1oz (25g) chopped angelica, 1oz chopped nuts (almonds, hazel or brazils), then turn into a baking tin lined with edible rice paper. Press and smooth down with a wet knife, then cover with another layer of rice paper and leave for at least 12 hours before cutting into bars.

Turkish Delight

Delicate and fragrant, these sugar-dusted cubes of Turkish delight in rose, orange, lemon, mint and pistachio flavours were first produced in the 17th century and are still made to the same time-honoured recipe. It was originally known as *lokum* but a 19th century British traveller gave this sweet confection the more familiar name.

Put 2lb (900g) sugar into a pan with ¼ pint (150ml) water. Dissolve 1oz (25g) gelatine in another ¼ pint (150ml) water, add to the mix, and boil for 20 minutes. Colour it pink with a drop of food colouring, then pour into wetted trays. Leave to set for 24 hours, then cut into squares and dredge with icing sugar

Savoury Sauces, Chutneys, Pickles and Jellies

Natural ingredients with spicy undercurrents set these savoury sauces, chutneys and pickles apart from their shop bought counterparts that are packed with preservatives and additives. Some, like mint sauce need no cooking, just pick a few stems of mint and pull off the leaves. Wash and chop finely then put in a sauce boat. Sprinkle 1 tablespoon of caster sugar over the mint then add 2-3 tablespoons of hot water to dissolve the sugar. Stir in 3-4 tablespoons of vinegar and use as an accompaniment to your lamb.

Certain sauces go in and out of fashion like the typically English salad cream that always smothered our salads as a child.

Salad Cream

Whip 2 eggs, add 2oz (50g) butter, 2 tablespoon sugar, ½ cup vinegar, ½ cup milk, salt and pepper to taste and beat well. Put into a double pan and heat, stirring all the time until the mixture thickens. Bottle. This will keep.

Salad Cream II

In a bowl, combine 1 dessertspoon flour, tablespoon dry mustard, tablespoon sugar, good pinch of salt and pepper, then add one whipped egg to make a stiff paste. Gradually add 3 tablespoons oil mixing all the time. Add ½ pint (275ml) milk, then ½ pint (275ml) white vinegar. Place the bowl in a pan of steadily boiling water and stir until the mixture thickens.

Salad Cream III

Put 2oz (50g) butter in a bowl over gently simmering water to melt, then add 2 teaspoons sugar, 1 teaspoon dry mustard, 1 egg, ¼ pint (150ml) vinegar, cup of milk or single cream. Cook until mixture thickens stirring all the time.

What a boost home made chutneys and pickles make to cold buffet fare or for a cheese board with a

Mint Sauce is easy to make and is a perfect accompaniment to lamb

difference. Made in small batches, you can use the ripest most succulent fruits and vegetables in season, simmered with spices. White vinegar gives a more attractive appearance, but brown vinegar has more flavour. Some pickle and chutney recipes call for brining of the vegetables. This draws out unnecessary moisture and keeps the vegetables crisp. To brine, dissolve 2oz (50g) cooking salt in every pint of water used and place the prepared vegetables in this for 24 hours. Rinse very thoroughly and dry gently.

If a recipe calls for spiced vinegar – place 2 pints (1.2 litres) of vinegar in a basin and add ¼oz (5g) cinnamon bark, ¼oz (5g) cloves, ¼oz (5g) mace, ¼oz (5g) whole allspice and a few peppercorns. Cover with a plate, stand the basin over a pan of water and steadily bring to the boil. Remove from heat and allow the spices to steep in the warm vinegar for 2 hours. Strain vinegar and use as required.

Elderberry Ketchup

Pack the elderberries into an ovenproof dish, cover with vinegar and put a lid on. Place in a slow oven for 2-3 hours to extract all the juice. Strain and measure the liquid while still hot, then pour into a pan. To every pint (568ml) liquor add 2oz (50g) cloves, ¼oz (5g) ground mace,

left and below: Before preparing the preserves make sure you have enough bottles and jars available. The old earthenware jars were the fore-runners of glass as they kept the contents from discolouring

½oz (10g) peppercorns, ¼oz (5g) allspice and 4 shallots. Boil until the liquor is well flavoured. Strain through muslin, add anchovy essence to taste and bottle at once. Seal tightly and allow to mature for 1-2 months. As elderberries are at their best in August, this sauce will be ready for those bonfire night celebrations.

Damson Chutney

This is a tangy chutney that goes well with mature cheese and crusty bread. These quantities make about 7lb (3kg) chutney.

Put 3lb (1.35kg) damsons in a preserving pan with 1 pint (570ml) vinegar and simmer until the fruit is soft enough to remove the stones. Discard these and to the damson fruit add 1½lb (675g) Bramley apples, peeled, cored and diced, 1lb (450g) onions, peeled and finely chopped, 2 teaspoons ground ginger, 3 level teaspoons salt and 1oz (25g) pickling spice (tied in muslin bag to handle of pan for easy removal later). Simmer until the mixture is soft, then add another pint (570ml) vinegar and 1lb (450g) soft, brown sugar, stirring well until the sugar has dissolved. Continue cooking and when the mixture is thick, remove from the heat and decant into warm jars, cover immediately with waxed discs and seal with clingfilm. Save the waxed

top and middle left: In Derbyshire the fruit of the elder grows prolifically
left: Elderberries can be used to make jelly, sauce and syrup

paper from cereal packets and cut into circles for covering. Do not use metal lids which may be affected by the acid content of the jelly. Leave for two months to mature.

Walnut Pickle

Pick the young wet walnuts while still green. They should be soft enough to pierce with a skewer or fork, so after pricking them lightly, drop them in a basin and pour over strong brine (salt water). Leave for about a week until they are quite black. Drain off the brine and wash, then allow to dry for a few days before packing into jars and covering with hot, pickling vinegar. Seal the jars and allow to stand for at least a month before eating.

Rowanberry Jelly

Rowan berries are too sour to be eaten raw, except by the birds, and should not even be tried as they contain parasorbic acid which causes indigestion and can lead to kidney damage. Heat treatment or freezing neutralizes this by changing it into the benign sorbic acid.

Rowan berries with the addition of apples or crab apples, to improve the set and the flavour, make an excellent jelly to serve with game, mutton, lamb and goose.

Strip the rowan berries from the branches using a fork until you have 1lb (450g) berries. Put into a pan with 1 chopped up apple, a few juniper berries, 3 cloves, a few mint leaves and 2¼ pints (1.3ml) water. Simmer for 45 minutes or until the fruit can be easily squashed with a potato masher. Allow to cool then tip into a jelly bag or muslin and leave to drain into a bowl overnight.

Next day measure the juice and add llb (450g) of preserving sugar to each pint of liquid. Heat gently to dissolve the sugar then boil hard for approximately 15 minutes and continue to boil until it sets when tested. Decant into warm jars, cover immediately with waxed discs and seal with clingfilm. Save the waxed paper from cereal packets and cut into circles for covering. Do not use

metal lids which may be affected by the acid content of the jelly. Store in a cool place for six months before using to allow the preserve to mature.

Rosehip Conserve

Rosehips are high in vitamin C but are often overlooked as fruits to preserve. To compensate, here is a delicious conserve that does not set solid but is full of fruit and is delicious eaten with savoury dishes. Put 2lb (900g) rose-hips, 6fl oz (175ml) malt vinegar, 10fl oz (275ml) water and ½ vanilla pod in a large pan. Simmer gently until the hips are completely soft. Pour into a jelly bag and allow to drain all night. To the juice add 1lb sugar and the juice of 1 lemon. Boil until the jam is set, then pot into sterile jars. If you use pot or china not glass it will stop the preserve loosing its beautiful tawny colour.

left (top to bottom): Rowan berries grow on the Mountain Ash tree. Strip the berries from the branches
top left: Put in a pan with apple, mint, cloves and juniper berries, and allow to simmer
left: Let the butler serve the Rowanberry Jelly which goes well with game, mutton, lamb and goose

Gran's Marrow Chutney

Cut a 4lb (1.8kg) marrow into small squares and lay in a brine of ½ cup salt to 3 pints (1.7ltr) water for 12 hours. Strain off and rinse well. Put 2 pints (1.2ltr) vinegar ½oz (10g) turmeric, ½oz (10g) ground ginger and 4oz (110g) sugar into a pan and boil for 10 minutes then add the marrow and boil for another ten minutes. Put into jars and use when cold. Gets better with keeping but guaranteed not to be around that long.

Marrow Pickle

Cut a 4lb (1.8kg) marrow and 1lb (450g) onions into small squares and lay in a brine of ½ cup salt to 3 pints (1.7ltr) water for 12 hours. Strain off and rinse well. Put 2 pints (1.2ltr) vinegar, 1 oz (25g) pickling spice and 1lb (450g) sugar into a pan and boil for 20-30 minutes. Thicken with a paste made of 1oz (25g) turmeric and 3oz (75g) flour mixed in a little cold water. Reboil. Put into jars and use when cold.

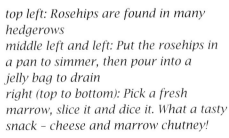

top left: Rosehips are found in many hedgerows
middle left and left: Put the rosehips in a pan to simmer, then pour into a jelly bag to drain
right (top to bottom): Pick a fresh marrow, slice it and dice it. What a tasty snack – cheese and marrow chutney!

Mustard Pickle - Piccalilli

Use seasonal vegetables such as cauliflower, gherkins, marrow, beans, cucumber and onions cut into very small pieces. Proportions of cauliflower should be double the other vegetables, so to one small cauliflower weighing about 1½lb (675g) add 12oz (350g) peeled, cubed marrow, ½ cucumber, 6oz (175g) onions, 2oz (50g) French beans. Aim for approximately 3-3½lb (1.35-1.6kg) fresh vegetables chopped very fine. Spice 1 pint (570ml) bottle of white vinegar with 1 teaspoon pickling spice ½ teaspoon ginger, pinch of salt and 1oz (25g) sugar. Pour over the vegetables and boil gently for 25 minutes or until all the vegetables are soft. Make a paste with one teaspoon of turmeric, 1 tablespoon flour and 1 tablespoon mustard mixed with a small amount of cold water. Add to the pickle and stir. Boil gently for another ten minutes, then allow to cool and bottle.

top left: To make mustard pickle, use seasonal vegetables like cauliflower, marrow, gherkins, beans, cucumber and onions
left: A jar of marrow chutney, a jar of mustard pickle and a jar of marrow and ginger preserve ready for the store cupboard
above: What a tasty snack – pork pie and mustard pickle

Jams and Preserves

Although its best to enjoy fruits and berries in season, the next best thing is to enjoy them all year round as preserves. Elderflowers, elderberries, blackberries, rowan berries, windberries (bilberries) are all available in the Derbyshire countryside and make excellent preserves.

To make perfect jam, fruit should be firm and fresh. Under-ripe fruit often lacks flavour, and over-ripe or damp fruit can prevent the jam from setting and cause it to go mouldy. As a guide, use 1lb (450g) sugar to 1lb (450g) fruit. The pectin or setting quality of fruit varies, so sometimes it is advisable to add lemon juice,

commercial pectin or more sugar to help the set. Use the following guide to decide the amount of sugar required for each pound of fruit, adding slightly more if the jam is to be kept.

A guide to the sugar content and cooking time of jams

Fruit	Quantity of sugar		Cooking time
	Imperial	Metric	
Cherries and black currants	12oz	350g	45 minutes
Plum	12oz	350g	25 minutes
Gooseberry	14oz	400g	40 minutes
Greengage	12oz	350g	25 minutes
Raspberry	14oz	400g	6 minutes
Red and white currants	14oz	400g	45 minutes
Quince	12oz	350g	30 minutes
Apricot	12oz	350g	25 minutes
Blackberry	12oz	350g	30 minutes
Strawberry	16oz	450g	6 minutes
Damson	16oz	450g	20 minutes
Rhubarb	16oz	450g	45 minutes
Marrow	16oz	450g	35 minutes

A guide to the sugar content and cooking time of jellies

Fruit	Quantity of sugar		Boiling time with sugar
	Imperial	Metric	
Blackberry	14oz	400g	20 minutes
Plum and apple	14oz	400g	15 minutes
Barberry	16oz	450g	10 minutes
Cranberry	16oz	450g	20 minutes
Gooseberry	16oz	450g	25 minutes
Quince	16oz	450g	25 minutes
Medlar	16oz	450g	90 minutes
Apple	16oz	450g	25 minutes

To make perfect jellies the table above is a guide to the amount of sugar required for each pint of fruit juice, and the length of time the juice should boil after the sugar is added.

Jam will contain approximately 60% sugar which means that 1lb (450g) sugar should yield 1²/₃lb (730g) jam; 3lb (1.35kg) sugar should yield 5lb jam (2.25kg) so make sure you have enough sterilised jars ready.

The secret of good jam is to allow the fruit to simmer very steadily to extract the pectin and soften the skin or peel. Add just sufficient liquid to cover the fruit, as a certain amount of evaporation must take place. Once the fruit is soft, the sugar is added. Let the sugar dissolve slowly as you stir it. Only then can you turn up the heat and let it boil rapidly. Stir it only occasionally, removing any scum with a metal spoon until it reaches setting point.

Use a sugar thermometer or alternatively test whether jam is set by dropping a small amount on a saucer. Allow it to cool then if the jam has set, it will wrinkle when pushed with your finger. Jam sets at 220°F – boiling water is 212°F so it's going to be bubbling away for quite some time before it reaches setting point. Here, alongside the sugar guide is a rough guide to the time that different fruits will need to boil before reaching setting point.

As with all jams, jellies, pickles and chutneys, when setting point is reached decant into warm, sterile jars, cover immediately with waxed discs, wax side down and seal with clingfilm. Save the waxed paper from cereal packets and cut into circles for covering. Do not use metal lids which may be affected by the acid content.

To give these delicious preserves as a special gift, first seal them with cling film, then use paper doyleys or make pretty paper circles for lids. Tie them with gold string, add a label and a personalised swing tab. For a gift selection, display as you would a flower arrangement in a sea grass gift basket, a willow woven flat bottomed basket, a trug, or a shallow box wrapped in cellophane and tied at the top with a big ribbon bow.

Apple and Ginger Jam

Peel and core cooking apples, then cut into neat cubes and weigh. Allow 1lb (450g) sugar for every 1lb (450g) of fruit. Place the apple cubes in a bowl, toss them in sugar and leave overnight. Place the peel and cores in a muslin bag and put these also in the bowl.

Remove the muslin bag and put the sugared apple into a strong pan. Simmer gently, stirring all the time until the sugar has dissolved. For every 1lb (450g) of apples, add 1 teaspoon ground ginger. Boil steadily until the jam sets when tested.

Marrow and Ginger Conserve

Peel a marrow. Cut in half lengthwise and remove the seeds and stringy parts. Cut the pulp into neat cubes and weigh. Allow 1lb (450g) sugar for every 1lb (450g) of pulp. Toss the marrow cubes and sugar into a pan, give them a stir, cover and leave overnight. The sugar will have turned to syrup. Simmer gently until the sugar has dissolved completely adding 1 teaspoon grated ginger root for every 1lb (450g) marrow pulp, plus the juice of one lemon, (4 lemons will be sufficient for 4lb–6lb (1.8kg-2.7kg) in weight) to improve the setting quality. Boil rapidly until the jam sets when tested.

This is a lovely lemon coloured conserve full of soft chunks. It is soft-set with a full-bodied flavour. It is fantastic on toast, but try it spooned over ice-cream, steamed pudding, fruit or combined with rhubarb in a crumble. It even makes a superb accompaniment for savoury dishes such as grilled pork or chicken. For an Asian twist, smother over fish and oven-bake in foil parcels.

Blackberry Jelly

Put 1lb (450g) blackberries, a teacup of water and 1 medium sized, cubed cooking apple, pips and peel too, into a pan. Simmer until soft. Use a

top left: The grated ginger root gives a delicious flavour to the marrow and ginger conserve
bottom left: Remove the skin of the marrow and dice
top right: Toss the marrow in sugar
above: Simmer gently then boil rapidly until the conserve sets when tested

potato masher to make a thick mush then strain through muslin. To extract the maximum juice, return the pulp to the pan, add another cup of water and bring to the boil again. After 15 minutes, strain again. Combine all the juice, measure and allow 1lb (450g) sugar to every pint. Put sugar and juice in a pan, heat gently, then boil rapidly until it sets when tested.

This is delicious on bread, scones, crumpet etc but have you ever thought of dropping a spoonful into a cup and adding freshly boiled water? It also makes an excellent fruity hot drink.

Windfall Jelly

This is one of the most economical jellies ever, because this recipe uses windfall apples or the apple peelings that would otherwise be thrown away.

Put the apple peelings into a stew pot, or wipe the windfalls and cut into chunks discarding any bad bruising or damage. Cover with water and stew gently in the oven for two hours. Allow to cool then strain. Put the juice into a pan and to each pint (570ml) of juice add the peel from one lemon and 1lb (450g) sugar. For extra flavour tie 6 or 7 cloves, a pinch of grated nutmeg and a small piece of stick cinnamon in piece of muslin and drop this in the

Blackberries are plentiful in the Derbyshire lanes. Add a chopped apple and simmer until soft, then strain through muslin before adding the sugar. Boil until setting temperature is reached

syrup. Heat gently to dissolve the sugar then boil hard for 20 minutes before testing. Continue to boil until it sets when tested.

Elderberry and Apple Jelly

The flowers and fruit of the elder tree are used in a number of recipes. As well as this recipes, in this book we have recipes for elderberry syrup and elderberry ketchup. Elderberries don't have the same fruity smell as blackberries but are equally delicious to taste.

Using a fork, pick elderberries from the stalks and measure. For 6 pints (3.5ltr) use 5lb (2.25kg) apples. For 1½ pints (850ml) use 1lb (450g) apples. Wipe the apples and cut into pieces without discarding either peel nor pips. Put in a pan with the elderberries. Using a potato peeler carefully remove the peel of 1 orange. Put it in a piece of tied up muslin with a stick of cinnamon and put with the apple and elderberries in the pan. Cover with about 1 pint (570ml) water and simmer gently until the fruits are pulp. Strain through a jelly bag and leave to drain overnight. Measure the juice and add 1llb (450g) sugar to each pint (570ml) juice. Heat gently until the sugar has melted then boil rapidly until it reaches setting point.

These are excellent economical jams, jellies and preserves that are ideal to

Strip the elderberries from their branches with a fork and put into a measuring jug

use up a glut of fruit like apples, vegetables like marrows or hedgerow freebies like blackberries, elderberries and rosehips. Using the same methods and the sugar/cooking chart on pages 105 and 106, these recipes can be adopted to make jams, jellies and preserves from plums, damsons, cherries, barberries, cranberries, medlars, black, red or white currants, gooseberries, greengages, raspberries, quince, apricots, strawberries and rhubarb. More traditionally oranges are made into marmalade and lemons into lemon curd.

Orange Marmalade

Wash and slice 1lb (450g) Seville or bitter oranges, extract the pips and tie them in a piece of muslin. Put everything into a pan, cover with 3 pints (1.7ltr) water and leave to stand overnight. Next day, simmer slowly for about 1½ hours until the peel is quite soft. Take out the bag of pips. Add 3lb (1.35kg) sugar and juice of 1 lemon. Heat gently until the sugar has melted then boil rapidly for about 20 minutes of until setting point is reached.

Lemon Curd

The zest is the coloured part of the orange or lemon peel that contains the oil that gives the characteristic flavour. Traditionally to extract this, cube sugar was rubbed over the peel and the sugar absorbed the oil. Alternatively, grate the peel of 3 large lemons taking care not to get the white pith, into a bowl. Add the freshly squeezed juice from the lemons, 10oz (527g) sugar and 4oz (110g) luxury butter. Place the bowl over a pan of gently boiling water stirring from time to time until the butter and sugar have completely melted. Add 2 well beaten eggs and continue cooking until the mixture is thick enough to coat the back of a spoon.

Extra Juicy James and Jellies

If you want to give your taste buds the red carpet treatment, how about using the same succulent fruit, laced with a generous measure of brandy, although sloe gin, whisky or rum can be substituted.

Carrot and Brandy Jam

Slice 4lb (1.8kg) carrots into thin slices, barely cover them with water and simmer steadily until tender, then mash. Add 4lb (1.8kg) sugar and bring slowly to the boil. Keep stirring and allow to boil for five minutes. Remove from heat and add the peel and juice of 1 lemon and 2 teaspoons of brandy. The brandy will not only give the jam a fantastic flavour, it will also help the jam to keep.

Waters and Wines

Derbyshire's White Peak is a dry land which gets its name from the bed of limestone rocks where falling rain is soaked up and disappears quickly to reappear as springs or wells, which materialize seemingly at random throughout the area. Settlements and farms clustered around the springs and wells, which were honoured with a pagan floral offering to the water god or spirit. This developed into the Derbyshire custom of Well Dressing which still persists in many Derbyshire villages as a floral tribute to the water spirit for providing the pure, clear water on which everything relied before the introduction of piped water last century.

It is almost impossible to date this well-dressing custom accurately, but we know that it took place in Tissington after the Black Death in 1350 when this Peakland village alone escaped the pestilence. The villagers immunity was almost certainly due to the purity of the water in their five wells. Now Tissington's well-dressing, held annually in May, heralds the start of the Well Dressing season.

The waters of Derbyshire have always been regarded as special and many villagers dropped new pins into their wells on Palm Sunday in thanks for a pure supply.

On Good Friday at Castleton drawn water from the well of Our Lady at the top of Cave Dale was mixed with liquorice then kept in a dark place until Easter Monday, when it was taken into the church and shaken during the service. This was a custom known as Shake-bottle.

At Tideswell on Easter Sunday, the water was embellished with sugar or honey, a custom known as sugar cupping. The water was collected from the Tor Spring at the foot of Dropping Tor.

A similar custom occurred at Chapel en le Frith on Whit Monday. Known

far left: Well-dressing at Tissington can be traced back to 1350
left: An old sign advertising Buxton's Well Dressings

as Bottle Day, the bottles were attached to string and slung round the necks of children. On Easter Monday the children went round with their bottles begging sugar from the local housewives.

Belper had a similar custom, but used mugs or bowls instead of bottles. Oatmeal and sugar was added to the water from the Lady's well, but on Easter Sunday at Bradwell, the children collected the water and drank it without additives.

Many places utilised this remarkable water for curative purposes. It was believed that anyone who drank the waters from the spring at Thirst House Cave in Deep Dale, south of King Sterndale, on Good Friday would have all their ailments cured.

More than one Derbyshire town grew on the fame of its healing waters, especially those where warm water bubbled up, if gases were present or the water was heavily mineralised. Despite the fact that many of these wells and springs are no longer in use, they have an interesting history.

Ashover water is chalybeate, a common expression for iron-bearing, with a reputation for flowing faster by night than by day. There are springs on private land. There is a road-side spring and a

thermal spring, situated in a wooded glen, but the water collects in a pool where it becomes brackenish.

Bakewell can trace its name back to Roman times when it was known as Beadaca's Well. Although the Duke of Rutland built a Bath House here in the 17th century, the town never became a fashionable place to take the waters.

Bradwell water was held in such high esteem that the Romans sent it out in barrels for the treatment of scrofula and other skin complaints.

Chesterfield has a number of streets with names like Beetwell Street, Spa Lane and Holywell Street. Holy wells, where miraculous cures were believed to take place, would face the east, presumably to the Holy Land.

Ilkeston waters had their origins in the coal measures. They are supposed to taste like Seltzer Water, as found at Selters in Germany, a form of soda water. A bath house was erected in 1830 on the present day Bath Street.

Kedleston water is a cool sulphur spring 47°F discovered in the park and duly enclosed in a fine structure. *'Efficacious in scorbutic and cutaneous diseases'* (scurvy and skin conditions), it was considered a remedy for gout and sold in the streets of Derby for that purpose.

Kedleston Hotel was built in expectation of the trade in visitors despite the fact that the waters stank horribly like bad-eggs.

Quarndon chalybeate spring lies on the road to Derby (SK333407) and is protected by a very attractive, three arched gothic structure. This ceased to flow after an earthquake in 1896, but sometimes a little water issues from the lion's mouth.

Stoney Middleton was known by the Romans. The spring is thermal at 64°F close to the west side of the church (SK232756). Reputed to have curative properties particularly for rheumatism. A crusader who returned from the Middle East with leprosy was supposedly cured by these waters. In gratitude he built the chapel dedicated to St Martin on which the present church is built.

Wirksworth once had a sulphur spring which Dr Short described *'Wirksworth black sulphur-water famous not only for Cutaneous disorders, but also for rheums of the eyes and Scrophulous Disorders...its water is very black'*.

Matlock – Dimple – a strong chalybeate spring at SK296604 is a mine sough driven into shale. It sits in a small garden with trees and shrubs. The water is channelled away but the degree of iron present can be seen by the heavy deposit of sinter on the channel and on articles left in the water.

Matlock Bath leapt to prominence when the railways reached there in 1848. Wealthy Victorians flocked to sample the medicinal waters and with its promenade atmosphere and blend of attractions, this picturesque inland resort soon developed into a fashionable spa town. The thermal spring that added the distinctive 'Bath' to Matlock still runs through a beautiful, public grotto just below Temple Road car park, marking the site of the first bath house built in 1698.

Certain Peak District warm springs encrust vegetation with their calcerous matter to form tufa. In other words, the mineralised thermal waters which are heavy with lime, deposit this onto moss which then decays to leave a spongy-looking stone behind. It's rather like the limescale build up in a kettle. This in turn supports more moss to be petrified so that tufa stone can 'grow' in banks up to twenty feet deep. Throughout the 19th century tufa was sold in great quantities, the perfect ornamental stone for romantic Victorian grottoes, arches and arbours. Tufa was quarried around Dunsley Springs, near Slaley, whilst at Matlock Bath vast amounts

left: The thermal spring that added the distinctive 'Bath' to Matlock still runs through a decorative public grotto and marks the site of the first bath house built in 1698
middle: The beautiful ceramic fountain that used to dispense water is now just for show
below: The heavily mineralised water of Matlock Bath, coats objects in a petrifying process

occur around hillside thermal springs.

Until recently, the water could still be taken at the Matlock Bath Pavilion, which houses the information centre and where the original drinking fountain can still be seen.

Just down the road from the Matlock Bath Pavilion is the former Matlock Bath Hydro, dating back to 1883 and now a popular tourist attraction called the Matlock Bath Aquarium. Here, the thermal pool is fed by a spring from the hillside gushing 600,000 gallons a day, at a constant temperature of 20°C. This is where patients would immerse themselves in the pool or take the waters to relieve rheumatic ailments and improve digestive disorders. Today the health giving properties of the water are enjoyed by a collection of Large Mirror, Common and Kai Carp, some weighing over 30lbs, and the former Victorian consulting rooms are now home to a selection of British and Tropical freshwater fish from Piranhas to Terrapins.

This is also one of the few places where you can still see the remarkable petrifying process at work. This was a source of curiosity and amazement visited by thousands of Victorian trippers to see the petrifying process actually taking place. At the working well in the Matlock Bath Aquarium the thermal water is sprayed onto objects, gradually turning them into stone.

Melbourne gets its name from Mel – sweet, or having the taste of honey, and burn – spring, and was once known as the *'Citie of Sweete Springes'*.

Ashbourne – It's not surprising that this special water should be sold commercially? A borehole at Ashbourne is the source of the bottled Ashbourne Water. The Nestle company searched the country for a suitable water and having decided on Ashbourne in the south-west of the county, launched their bottled water in 1976, as a limited trial. Within 5 years it had captured 30% of the United Kingdom market of 40 million litres, nearly 9 million gallons per year.

Buxton – Possibly the best known Derbyshire water is that which is bottled in Buxton. The Romans called the town *Aquae Arnemetiae* and used it as one of their watering holes, yet Arnemetis was the name of a Celtic goddess which would suggest pre-Roman influence. Buxton became famous as a healing place and spa. It attracted visitors from all parts of the country including Mary Queen of Scots who took the waters daily on her visits.

During her twelve years in Derbyshire she stayed in Buxton on six occasions, and after a five week reside in the summer of 1573, she wrote to thank Queen Elizabeth for agreeing to her visit to Buxton, saying she had been 'afforded some relief'.

During the 18th century, the gouty, greedy and self-indulgent 'took the water' at Buxton, and although it is no longer a fashionable spa town or centre for religious pilgrimages for the sick and inform, its waters are still believed to be medicinal and plans are afoot to reinstate the town and return it to its former glory.

For those who can't get to Buxton, its water is now bottled and sold throughout the world. The supply comes from the spring under the 1853, Natural Baths building but the same supply that fills the bottles of Buxton Water is available free at the pump in the centre of the town opposite The Crescent. The water is luke warm and has no unpleasant taste. You can drink as much as you like and people fill bottles to take home. I asked if there was any difference between this and the commercially bottled water and was told categorically no, but because a sediment would collect in the bottom of the bottles, for aesthetic purposes this is filtered before bottling.

Traditional 'Still' Lemonade

The quintessentially English drink for a hot afternoon in the garden.

Traditionally, to extract the lemon zest, the coloured part of the orange or lemon peel that contains the oil that gives the characteristic flavour, sugar cubes were rubbed over the peel to absorbed the oil. Alternatively, grate the peel of 3 large lemons, or use a potato peeler for speed, taking care not to get the white pith, into a bowl or large heat proof jug. Add 6oz (175g) sugar and pour on 1½ pints (850ml) boiling water. Cover and leave to cool, stirring occasionally. Add the juice of the lemons. Strain the lemonade and serve chilled.

far left: The statue of Arnemetiae, a Celtic Water Goddess worshipped at Buxton (Buxton Museum)
middle and left: The modern day well at Buxton is dedicated to St Anne and its still possible to take the waters
above: If you can't get to Buxton, you can buy the bottled water

For something slightly different, add a handful of raspberries to the mix to make Pink Lemonade.

Lemon and Barley Water

In the rural calendar, July is the month for haymaking – a time when farmers took on extra staff and provided them with meals and refreshing drinks while they mowed and gathered the hay. Farmer's wives made their own drinks to take out to the men in the fields and, whether alcoholic or non-alcoholic, they all had a certain amount of nutritional value. One such drink was barley water which has been used since Neolithic times as both a medicine and a refreshment. The cooling properties in barley when made into a drink, are known for easing digestive problems and fevers. When applied to the skin as a poultice, it calmed bites, cooled rashes and helped heal wounds.

Early recipes for barley water were mixed with honey, later it was flavoured with liquorice and it wasn't until the 1600s that lemons were used. It became known locally as Chaddesden barley water. Derbyshire author Alison Uttley told how they made large amounts of Chaddesden barley water and sent it up to the men in the fields, adding that a drink of barley water was also given to the horses as a treat.

Put 1 teaspoon pearl barley into a saucepan, cover with cold water and bring to the boil. Strain off the water and throw it away. Rinse the barley under cold, running water, then return to the saucepan. This makes the resultant drink less cloudy. Add one pint (570ml) water and the peel of a lemon. Bring to the boil. Cover and simmer for an hour, strain the liquid into a jug or large basin, add one tablespoon sugar and the juice of a lemon. Allow to cool before drinking.

Slackers

One of the best, non-alcoholic beverages, highly rated by workmen for its thirst quenching and nutritional values, was a drink called 'slackers' which got its name from its ability to slack your thirst. Also known as stokos, it was made up of fine oatmeal and water, sweetened with either lump sugar or honey.

Slice 1 lemon and put in a pan with ¼lb fine oatmeal and 6oz sugar. Mix together with a little warm water, then add a gallon of boiling water, stir thoroughly, cool and serve.

left: Traditional still lemonade, the quintessential English drink for a hot afternoon

Flummery or Flummerty or Frummenty

As the reaping machines went round the fields cutting the corn and tying it into bundles with binder twine, the men followed picking up the bundles and putting them into shocks, which were left to dry before being taken and packed into the Dutch Barns – sheds with roofs but no sides. When the corn was all cut, the village folks went with bags picking up loose cornstalks that had been left. This was known as gleaning. Folks used their gleanings to feed fowls, had it ground into flour or made it into Flummery.

The grain would be covered with water and kept warm for 2 days to 'cree' during which time, they would swell, soften and jell. They would then be boiled in sweetened milk flavoured with spices, and either eaten as a pudding or consumed as a thick, creamy drink.

Blackberry Cordial
August/September

Put 5lb (2.25kg) blackberries, clean and whole into a large pan. Add 2oz (50g) citric acid, add water to cover. Stir frequently but without breaking or bruising the fruit or the cordial will be dull. Cover and leave to steep overnight. Next day, strain the juice into a clean pan and to every pint of juice add 1½lb (675g) preserving sugar. Heat gently, stirring to dissolve the sugar, bring to the boil and boil for 10 minutes. Leave to cool, then strain into clean, screw topped bottles. Dilute to taste.

Elderflower Fizz   May/June

Pick 4 large heads of elderflower. Don't wash them, but remove any insects and the thick stalks. Put 1½lbs (675g) granulated sugar in a very large bowl and cover with 2 pints (1.2ltr) boiling water. Stir until the sugar has dissolved, then add 6 pints (3.5ltr) cold water, the rind and juice of 2 large lemons, 2 tablespoons white wine vinegar and the elderflowers. Stir well, cover and leave for 48 hours, stirring occasionally. Strain through a fine sieve into clean bottles with pop-off caps, leaving an inch gap at the top of each bottle. Store in a cool place to mature for 6 weeks, when it will be ready to drink.

Elderberry Syrup   September

Pick elderberries from the stalks and measure. Put in a large pan with ½ pint (275ml) water for every 2 pints (1.2ltr) berries, simmer until all the juice is extracted then strain through a jelly bag. Measure the juice and to each 2 pints (1.2ltr) add ½oz (10g) cloves, ½oz (10g) root ginger 1 stick cinnamon bark all well bruised and tied in a bag. Add 1lb (450g) sugar, boil for 15 minutes, strain and bottle when cold. Dilute with hot or cold water.

Rosehip Syrup

One of natures pick-me-ups is the rose-hip, fruit of the dog-rose, boiled to make an invigorating syrup and now known to be packed with vitamin C.

Remove the leaves, stalks and calyces from 1lb (450g) ripe rosehips. Wash, mince or liquidize. Pour one pint of boiling water into a pan and add the rosehips. Bring to the boil, give a good stir, then remove from the heat and set aside for 15 minutes before straining through muslin. To extract the maximum juice, return the pulp to the pan, add another ½ pint (275ml) water and bring to the boil again. After 15 minutes, strain again. Pour all the juice into a clean pan, and reduce until it measures about ½ pint (257ml) then add 6oz (175g) sugar. Heat gently to allow the sugar to melt, then boil rapidly for 3-5 minutes. Pour into hot, sterile bottles, cork and cool. Poor keeping quality – once opened use within a week

Soda Water

Boil 3 pints (1.7ltr) water and allow it to go cold. Add 12oz (350g) sugar, 1oz (25g) tartaric acid and juice of ½ lemon. Beat the whites of 1 egg and add to the liquid. Mix well and bottle. According to gran's recipe *'For a drink put two tablespoons in a tumbler of cold water with a quarter of a teaspoon of bicarbonate of soda which will make it effervesce.'* A more modern drink would be a spritzer – half a tumbler of soda water to half a tumbler of cold white wine.

Rosehips are well known for their health giving properties and make a tasty drink

Temperance Drink

To every 8 pints (4.5ltr) elderberries add 6 pints (3.5ltr) water. Let it stand for three days then strain through a sieve, pressing the berries to extract all the juice. To each 2 pints (1.2ltr) liquid add 1lb (450g) sugar Put 1oz (25g) ginger and 1oz (25g) bruised cloves into a muslin bag. Put everything into a pan and boil gently for an hour. Strain into a clean vessel and when cool add one tablespoon yeast. Leave to ferment for three days, then skim and bottle. Cork tightly and leave for three weeks before serving.

Home Made Ginger Beer

Periodically the craze for making ginger beer results in a chain of people trying to unload their 'ginger beer plants' on neighbours and friends, so don't try this unless you really love ginger beer. These 'plants' multiply faster than rabbits.

To start your 'ginger beer plant', blend 2oz (50g) fresh baker's yeast with 2 tablespoons caster sugar until they cream and form a liquid. Add 2 tablespoons ground ginger and ½ pint (275ml) water. Stir well and place the liquid in a covered jar with a loose lid.

Each day – add one level teaspoon dried ginger and one level teaspoon caster sugar to 'the plant' and stir well.

After ten days – dissolve 18oz (500g) caster sugar in 1½ pints (850ml) water and bring to the boil. Cool slightly then add the strained juice of two lemons.

Strain the 'ginger beer plant' through a sieve and add the strained liquid to the sugar and lemon juice together with 6 pints (3.5ltr) water. Stir well and bottle at once in strong, screw-topped bottles. Store in a cool place and use as required.

To make more, half the 'plant' (the sediment left in the sieve) and place in two separate jars. Add ½ pint (275ml) water, 2 level teaspoons ground ginger and 2 level teaspoons caster sugar to each jar, stir and give one to a friend. Feed daily as above for 10 days, then siphon off and split again. Continue indefinitely.

Posset

Posset was a favourite Derbyshire drink consumed on Christmas eve, or given as an aphrodisiac to newly weds on their wedding night.

It is a mixture of boiled milk or cream, eggs, ale, treacle/syrup, ginger, nutmeg and other spices.

The medicinal properties of posset were well documented during the Eyam Plague of 1665 when the entire Derbyshire village isolated itself to prevent the infection spreading.

When the plague arrived at the village of Eyam, as depicted in this magnificent 'Plague Window', posset was given as a remedy. An annual, open-air service is still held to commemorate the sacrifice made by the people of Eyam

Reverend Mompesson obtained a supply of the best remedies then in vogue and amongst them was posset. Apparently after drinking this medicinal brew, Marshall Howe, who later set himself up as the self appointed undertaker and sexton, was one of those who successfully recovered. The drooping spirits of the people of Eyam must have been lifted considerably on hearing that posset had effected a cure, although sadly in the majority of cases it was ineffective.

Alison Uttley wrote – *'We had possets at Christmas, at New Year, when we were ill and when we were starved.'* (a Derbyshire expression meaning frozen stiff from the weather, not dying of hunger). Children had a posset of hot milk and bread cut into little squares, with a dash of rum and brown sugar. Men had stronger possets to revive them. The posset was mulled on the hot stove and the custom was so widespread even Shakespeare mentioned it when he wrote *'We will have a posset at the end of a sea-coal fire.'* We had possets by our own coal fire from the coal dug in our own county.

Posset pots and caudle cups were made extensively in earthenware in the 1600s to hold these warm drinks. Posset was drunk from a special posset pot which, like the loving cup, had two handles, one on each side to enable the heavy pot to be passed from one person to another. Caudle cups had either one or two handles and some had lids and saucers too. In Eyam Museum there is a posset cup that belonged to the late Clarence Daniel, Eyam antiquary who stated the museum. His ancestors survived the plague and this cup could date back to those dark days of 1665.

Caudle

A warm drink of thin, spiced gruel mixed with wine or ale that was considered highly beneficial for invalids. It had the addition of oatmeal as well as the eggs, sugar, spices, wine and ale.

From this comes the word 'coddle', the culinary method of gently steaming or boiling, and 'mollycoddle' which means to indulge or pamper. The 'molly' half is used to describe an effeminate man.

Jane Mosley's hand written recipe from 1690

To Make A Caudle

Take Ale the quantity that you mean to make and set it on the fire, and when it is ready to boil, scum it very well, then cast in a large mace, and take the yolks of 2 eggs for 1 mess or one drought and beat them well, and take away the skin of the yolks, and then put them into the ale, when it seetheth. Be sure to stir them well till it seeth again for a youngling, then let it boil a while and put in your sugar, and if it be to eat cut three or four toasts of bread thin, and toast them dry but not brown, and put them to the Caudle, if to drink put none.

Posset cup

Nutmeg

The habit of grating nutmeg onto food or drinks became such a widespread fashion in the 19th century that people carried a nutmeg and a small nutmeg grater in their pocket or bag. It was believed to aid digestion and avoid the problem of flatulence. Taken regularly it was said to counter problems like lumbago, rheumatism and headaches.

Ponado

Another popular drink of the era was Ponado or ponada, a thick drink made by boiling bread in flavoured water to obtain a pulp.

Jane Mosley's hand written recipe from 1690

To Make A Ponado

The quantity you will make set on in a posnet (a small metal pot with a handle and three feet) of faire water, when it boils, put a mace in, and a little piece of cinnamon, and so much bread as you think meet, so boil it and season it with salt, sugar and rose water and so serve it.

Syllabub

Originally a festive drink made from fresh milk and wine, ale or cider which gradually evolved into a dessert. It became very popular in the 18th century.

Advocaat

Also known as egg-nog and egg-flip, this recipe is 32 degree proof strength and is an excellent pick-me-up for invalids.

Beat 3 egg yolks, then gradually add ½ pint (275ml) evaporated milk or cream beating all the time until well blended. Beat in ¼ pint (150ml) sugar syrup, ¼ pint (150ml) rum or brandy and finally a teaspoon of the vanilla essence. Bottle when it is the consistency that will only just pour.

Derbyshire Ale

When it was unsafe to drink water, ale was the alternative and an average consumption was 4 pints (2.25ltr) of ale per person per day.

Ale was made to raise money. At Whitsuntide, many churches offered to their parishioners ale brewed by the verger and clergy in exchange for money to repair the church roof or similar needs. In the Bodleian Library is a record of Whitsun Ales at Elvaston and Ockbrook, showing that these two places were each required to brew 4 ales of a quarter of malt. Each husband and wife must pay 2d and every cottager a penny.

The word bridal comes from bridale – the ale made by the engaged couple (or more probably the bride-to-be) to sell to their friends and family at their wedding nuptials. Everyone was invited to participate in the celebrations and gave willingly as they drank the health of the newly married couple. Now all we are left with is the name bridal which is hitched to anything pertaining to the bride – the bridal bed, the bridal cars, bridal flowers etc.

Many farm houses brewed ales, and before regulated licensing, any householder could brew and sell ale. Up to the 16th century, English ale was made only of malted barley, but the housewives who in those days were the brewers, would make beer from local herbs or add them to the ale to give it extra flavour.

Pub Signs

Unsurprisingly, some form of regulation was needed and as long ago as the thirteenth century, the law demanded that a pole projected from the wall of an ale house to indicate that a new brew had been made so that the authorities could check it. As taverns and ale-houses multiplied, it was necessary for them to identify themselves, and what more convenient than a sign hanging from this pole. This was the beginning of pub signs.

Usually the sign and name of an inn would reflect some local tradition, the reigning monarch, a past activity or the name of the local squire who probably owned the place. There are now fewer and fewer traditional names being used, and lesser known ones that might have some obscure meaning are fast disappearing. One such name is 'The Chequers', with inns at Calver and Dronfield. The explanation for the use of this name and the chequer board as a tavern sign relates to the use of local herbs and berries that were added to the brew. In this case, it was the native berries from the wild service tree whose furrowed bark develops a characteristic square pattern leading to the nick-name 'chequer tree'.

Very few inns derive their name from the speciality of the house, but those that do hold a few appetising surprises. The Cheshire Cheese at Hope is a 16th century overnight stopping place on the Transpennine Salt route, when payment for lodgings was actually made in cheese. The original cheese hooks are still to be seen

Names like The White Horse, The Coach and Horses, and The Old Nag's Head, usually indicated that livery stables were once associated with the tavern. The Packhorse Inn at

Little Longstone was originally built as a pair of lead miners cottages in the early 17th century. It has been a pub since the 1780s, and the speciality of the house is Packhorse Pie – named after the packhorse route that went past the door, not the pie filling.

What could be more appealing than to slack your thirst at The Barrel Inn at Chesterfield; Brewers Fayre at Barlborough; The Punch Bowl at Chesterfield, The Jug and Glass at Worksop and Lea, or The Vine Inn at Worksop.

As a tribute to the hardwork of the farming community we find The Jolly Farmer at Dronfield Woodhouse and Holmwood; The Farmyard at Youlgreave; The Plough at Hathersage and Low Bradfield; and The Wheatsheaf at Newbold

There's The Market Inn at Chesterfield; The Gardners at Clay Cross; The Peak Pantry at Eyam; The Dusty Miller at Barlborough; and The Beehive at Harthill.

Moving into the food chain we find The Butcher's Arms at Brimington; The Bull's Head at Monyash, Holymoorside and Foolow; The Black Bull at Bolsover

The fact that Derbyshire is a sheep farming county is reflected in The Derby Tup at Whittington Moor; The

Fleece at Holme; The Golden Fleece at Chesterfield; The Shoulder of Mutton at Bradwell and Hardstaff; and The Lamb at Holymoorside. Strangely there is no reference to pigs or cows.

There's the game element with The Dog and Partridge at Thorpe; The Grouse Inn at Chesterfield; and The Fox and Goose at Wigley.

The fishermen haven't been forgotten. There's The Lazy Trout at Meersbrook; The Riverside at Ashford in the Water; The Angler's Rest at Bamford and the Tickled Trout at Barlow. Almost at the confluence of the Rivers Dove and Manifold is The Isaak Walton Hotel named after a self-educated iron-monger who moved to the area after retirement. He spent his days fishing and inspired by his beloved Dovedale, wrote a book called *The Complete Angler*. It was so popular, there were five editions during his lifetime, (1593-1683) and it's still available. It gained Isaac Walton the title 'father of all anglers'. Further up stream at Hartington is The Charles Cotton, named after a country gentleman, owner of Berrisford Hall (now a ruin), and fishing friend of Isaak Walton. Charles Cotton (1630-1687) – known as the 'Laureate of the Dove' contributed to the second part of Isaac Walton's book *The Complete Angler*.

Testing The Ale

Ale conners – testers – are said to have judged the quality of the ale by pouring some on the bench and sitting in the puddle in leather breeches for half an hour. If the testers britches were semi-stuck to the seat, then the brew was deemed satisfactory but if they stuck, the ale was considered to have been adulterated by the addition of sugar.

In 1995, in Fenny Bentley, two miles from Ashbourne and the most southern village in the Peak District, the quaintly named Leatherbritches Brewery was launched at the Bentley Brook Inn, on the south side of the village. The brewery name originated from that long ago practice of sitting in a pool of ale.

By the 18th century, beer and ale had come to mean the same thing in Britain. It was in the 15th century that some experimenters began adding hops to ale. The hops were referred to as pernicious weeds despite the fact that hops are actually a wild herb that is now widely cultivated for beer making. For nearly 100 years drinkers opposed this new-fangled notion of adding a strange aromatic flower to their brew, but in the end the hops won and beer took over from ale. The hops added not only an extra flavour but a preservative quality so the beer could be kept longer.

Mulled Ale

This is a traditional 18th century version for those who have a poker handy. Unlike the modern version of mulled ale, this recipe requires the addition of eggs.

Heat 2 pints (1.2ltr) ale, grated rind ½ lemon, 1 level teaspoon ground ginger and 1 level teaspoon ground nutmeg. Bring to near boiling point. Meanwhile make a poker red-hot; plunge it into the ale and hold it there until the seething stops. Whip 3oz (75g) soft brown sugar with 3 eggs until frothy. Warm ¼ pint (150ml) brandy and ¼ pint (150ml) rum together in another small pan, combine with the egg mixture and pour into the ale mixture. Whisk until smooth and creamy, then serve.

Dr Johnson's Choice of Mulled Wine

This is the classic 18th century mulled wine recipe which Derbyshire can lay claim to as Dr Samuel Johnson, compiler of the celebrated *English Dictionary*, regularly stayed with his life-long friend Dr John Taylor at The Mansion, Church Street, Ashbourne. There is a plaque outside the building with the details *'Dr John Taylor was visited by Dr Samuel Johnson at this house 1740-1784'.*

right: A glass of mulled wine, offers a welcoming, warm drink
below: Rhubarb juice added to white wine makes a great cocktail

Pour 1 bottle red wine into a saucepan with 12 lumps sugar and 6 cloves. Bring to near boiling point, then add 1 pint (570ml) boiling water. Pour in ¼ pint (150ml) curacao and ¼ pint (150ml) brandy. Pour into glasses and grate nutmeg on top.

Our Family Favourite Mulled Wine

Into a medium pan pour 1 bottle red wine and drop in 6 cloves, a pinch of ginger, a cinnamon stick and 1½ tablespoons brown sugar. Heat gently. Add a cup of black tea, ½ cup water, ½ cup orange juice, 1 tablespoon brandy, and 1 tablespoon port. When pleasantly warm, ladle into glasses.

Lambs Wool

A hot, spiced ale popular in the Middle Ages. The name comes from the fluffy white flesh which bursts through the skins of the roasted apples which float on top.

Place 4 russet eating apples in a dish with a little cider, ale or water in a moderate oven and cook for 30 minutes until the apple flesh is 'woolly' in texture.

Meanwhile in a large pan, gently heat 4 pints (2.25ltr) ale or cider, 6 cloves, 1 teaspoon of grated nutmeg, ½ teaspoon ground ginger, 3 allspice berries, 1 broken cinnamon stick and 1-2 tablespoons dark, soft brown sugar. Do not allow to boil. Strain into a large serving bowl. With a spoon, scoop out the apple pulp. Discard the pips and core, and pile on the hot ale. Serve hot with a scoop of apple flesh in each glass. This should be eaten with a spoon.

Wassail Punch
Served at Christmas and New Year

A hot, spiced drink that takes its name from the Anglo Saxon toast *'Waes Hael'* or *'to your health'*. This greeting was called out by the Saxon overlord of the household when he bade everyone drink from the large wooden bowl kept especially for the purpose. After the master had drunk, the bowl would be passed round the household for everyone to 'sup' from a sizeable communal spoon.

From this developed the custom of the peasants going round with an empty wassailing bowl at Christmas, begging for food and drink to fill it. It was considered very bad luck not to contribute something to the wassailers.

Those carrying the wassailing bowl would sing a song outside each house –

Here we come a-wassailing
Among the leaves so green
Here we come a-wassailing
So fair to be seen

God bless the master of this house
Likewise the mistress too
And all the little children
That round the table go

Good master and good mistress
While sitting round your fire
Pray think of us poor children
Who are wandering in the mire

Put 4 small, eating apples with 2 cloves stuck in each, in an ovenproof dish in a low oven, and pour 8oz (225g) soft, brown sugar over them. Pour in 1 pint of medium sherry and 1 cinnamon stick and bake for 20 minutes or until the apples are just beginning to soften and brown. Do not overcook. Transfer the contents to a large saucepan and pour in 4 pints (2.25ltr) brown ale with the thinly pared rind of 2 oranges. Heat until it just begins to simmer, then serve in heatproof glasses.

Haddon Hospitality

At every level of society, Christmas has always been recognised as an occasion for music, mirth and merriment, gaiety, greetings and goodwill.

The atmosphere of festive cheer was definitely abundant at Haddon Hall, the Derbyshire seat of the Earls of Rutland, where it was best not to refuse the Earl's hospitality or suffer the consequences. One curious relic of social history which is attached to the wainscoting in the banqueting hall is an iron manacle. It is said that any guest who did not drink fair was liable to have his hand fixed in the manacle, and the drink he had not taken was then poured down his sleeve.

Letters in a Barrel

It could be said that the ill fated Mary Queen of Scots owes her downfall to Derbyshire ale. It's a well documented story that while under house arrest at Tutbury Castle she secretly smuggled out letters to her Catholic sympathisers in empty beer barrels. What isn't so well known is that the ale for Tutbury castle, which lies just over the Derbyshire border,

was brewed at Hilton, Derbyshire, eight miles south-west of Derby on the old Derby to Uttoxeter road. The brewery is no longer there, but the building which dates from 1520 and is Grade II listed is now the Old Talbot Inn. There are the remnants of a malt-drying kiln from its days as an alehouse on the back of the main fireplace.

In those long ago days when Queen Mary was imprisoned at various stately homes dotted around the area, many of her supporters tried to devise ways of freeing her and establishing her on the English throne. Queen Elizabeth was well aware of this and with her spy catcher Sir Francis Walsingham was constantly on the look out for any pending trouble and evidence of the Queen's complicity. Walsingham persuaded Gilbert Gifford, who had formerly been a staunch Catholic supporter turned traitor, to insinuate himself into the queen's household and then into her confidence. Because her rooms were regularly searched and her letters stolen, it was at Gifford's suggestion that a brewer who made regular deliveries of beer to the castle should carry secret messages to and from Queen Mary in a watertight barrel.

It could be said that Mary Queen of Scots owes her downfall to Derbyshire Ale

Having tricked Queen Mary into thinking this was a safe way to communicate with her loyal supporters, unsurprisingly the messages were intercepted by a cipher expert who immediately sent all the coded messages to Walsingham who didn't have to wait long before a letter from Anthony Babington came to light. The handsome heir to considerable estates, Anthony Babington belonged to an old Catholic family from Dethick in Derbyshire. His letters were enough to denounce him, so not only was his fate sealed, so too was that of the unfortunate Queen.

Herbal Beer

Wine and beer has been brewed in the home since time immemorial. Until the last century, it was still quite common for herbal beers to be made every spring in country homes. Winter diets needed a spring-time pick-me-up and these beers were given to all comers with the remark, *'This will clear your blood after the long winter'.*

Herbal beer is a term usually applied to beers made with herbs other than hops. Herb beers are a refreshing drink and have the advantage of being ready in a few weeks. They also use familiar weeds that grow abundantly almost anywhere, the most popular being nettles and dandelions. Nettle beer is made using the fresh tips of orchard grown nettles, a wonderful source of iron and vitamin C. Herb beer also contained a large quantity of nettles, plus a mixture of other garden herbs like sage, mint, dandelion root or yarrow. Unlike other home-made beers, these were ready to drink in a matter of days rather than months, so they were always available to serve to visitors and farm-workers alike. Until sanitation improved, it was safer to drink beer rather than plain water as the water had been sterilised in the brewing process.

Equipment is minimal – a 1 gallon polythene bucket with lid (cling-film or similar can act as a substitute), a pan big enough to boil the herbs, a fine sieve or piece of fabric and clean beer bottles.

Nettle Beer

Using rubber gloves and scissors, gather fresh, young nettle shoots. If the plant is older, take only the top two or three pairs of leaves for best results, but ignore any that have formed flower heads as they are too bitter to use.

Wash 1½ lb (675g) nettles and put them in a 1 gallon (4.5ltr) polythene bucket. Add 2 sticks of rhubarb – broken and bruised, and the peel and zest of 1 lemon. Pour on 1 gallon boiling water and leave to stand. When almost cold, strain. To the liquid add 12oz (350g) sugar and when dissolved, add 1 teaspoon ginger and the juice from the lemon. Mix well together. Cream 1oz (25g) yeast and add to the liquid. Leave to stand for 12 hours. Skim off the foam and bottle in strong bottles. The beer can be drunk one hour after bottling.

Dandelion Beer

Dig up the whole dandelion plant, flowers, leaves, taproot and all. Wash carefully and remove any dead leaves. You will need 2lb (900g) of dandelion plants. Pull them apart and place in a large pan with 1oz (25g) root ginger. Pour over boiling water and simmer for 5-10 minutes. When cool drain the dandelion water into a clean vessel and to extract the full flavour, squeeze the pulp before discarding. To remove any bits, sieve through a piece of muslin or similar. The dandelion water is now ready to make the beer.

Add 2lb (900g) malt extract, ½lb (225g) sugar, juice from ½ lemon, and ¼ teaspoon salt. Stir thoroughly and make the quantity up to 1 gallon (4.5 litres) with more water. Cool to between 18-20° Centigrade or 65-70° Fahrenheit and stir in the ale yeast according to the manufacturers instructions. Put the brew into a fermentation vessel with a well-fitting lid. Maintain this temperature and keep covered for 4-7 days to allow to ferment, but if necessary, remove the yeast from the top at intervals. When fermentation has finished the liquid looks clear and bubbles cease to rise. Siphon the beer into another clean container.

Dissolve 1¾oz (50g) sugar in a small quantity of hot water and add to the beer. Siphon into clean beer bottles and stopper down well. Store in a warm room for two days, then transfer to a cool place and store for at least two weeks before drinking. The flavour of the beer will improve during the following month.

Dandelion Wine

Gather 4 pints (2.25ltr) dandelion flowers on a sunny day. Put them in a pan with 1 gallon (4.5litre) cold water and bring to the boil, simmer for 10 minutes. This is known as the 'must'. Strain the 'must' onto 3½lb (1.6kg) sugar. Add the thinly peeled rind of 1 lemon and 1 orange. Stir well. When luke warm, add the juice of the orange and lemon, and the wine yeast (see manufacturers instructions for quantities) mixed with a little of the liquid. Yeast is essential for the fermentation to take place. Without yeast there would be no wine. Cover the 'must' with a cloth. Do not seal it with cling film or a tight fitting lid as the yeast needs oxygen which it can absorb from the air. Leave in a warm place for two to five days until fermentation begins, then strain and transfer the 'must' to a narrow necked vessels, cask or fermenting jar which should be tightly corked and fitted with an air lock. During fermentation the yeast is breaking down the sugar, forming alcohol and carbon dioxide. The air lock will permit the carbon dioxide from the fermenting liquor to escape, but will not allow air to enter the fermenting jar. This is important as the entry of air will turn the 'must' into vinegar instead of wine.

Keep the 'must' slightly warm then fermentation will be steady and continue for several weeks. Fermentation ceases when all the sugar has been used up or when the alcohol content is so high that the yeast dies. When the wine has settled, siphon it off the sediment at the bottom of the jar into a clean jar or container and seal again. This is known as racking off. Leave undisturbed to allow the wine to clear, then siphon into sterilised wine bottles and cork. Store in a cool place for around six months before sampling.

Vegetable Marrow Wine

Wipe the marrow with a clean, damp cloth, then slice it up into small pieces. Put the skin, pulp and seeds into a large bowl or sterile bucket. Add peel and zest of 2 lemons and 1 orange, 1oz (25g) ginger and 6oz (175g) chopped raisins. Pour on 1 gallon (4.5ltr) boiling water, stir thoroughly and when cool add the juice of the 2 lemons and the orange, nutrient and Sauterne yeast. Ferment on the pulp for 4 days pressing it down and agitating the mixture twice daily. Strain, stir in 2½lb (1.1kg) sugar and continue the fermentation in a narrow necked vessels, cask or fermenting jar which should be tightly corked and fitted with an air lock.

Keep the 'must' slightly warm and proceed as for Dandelion Wine.

Jane Mosley's hand written recipe from 1690

To Make Raison Wine (translation of old text)

Take six pound of raisons, 2 quarts of water well boyld as long as any skum is to be taken of(f) as it riseth. Your raisons must be well washed and stoned and put into a pot that hath a Spigot and forset and two lemons and one pound of lompe sugar. Take one rine of(f) and put them both in the pot thin sliced and put the water boyling hot upon these before named and let it stand 4 or 5 dayes. Then draine it thoroug a haire sive and when it is cleare bottle it up with a pound of lump sugar, into every bottle 2 or 3 lumps. This is the true way to make Couslip wine also. You may set your bottles when filed two or three days in the sun. This I have seen Mrs Powell doe. You may try som soe and put them in a sellar after with the rest.

Jane Mosley's hand written recipe for Raison Wine & Cherry Wine

Jane Mosley's hand written recipe from 1690

To Make Cherry Wine (translation of old text)

Take 5 pounds of sugar, one quart of water. Boyle it a little. Skum it cleane. Then put in 14 pounds of cherrys stoned besides the iuyce that comes from them. Boyle them for three quarters of an houre; skum them often and cover them as the boyle with a long sheet of white paper that the sugar may boyle all over them. Then powder them into earthen pans and let them stand 24 hours. After, take out the cherrys and put them upon sives to draine for 6 hours; then strow loafe sugar fine beaten on the toppes of the sives you dry them upon and lay the cherrys on. The strew sugar upon the cherrys. Dry them in the son and turn them som times; the juyce from which you take your cherrys that is to make your wine. It must stand in the pans for 8 or 10 dayes. Then strain it through a hipachrist bagg into a small runlett or bottles every night and morning till the wine hath done working and be very cleare on the top. Then stop it lose and keep it in a cool cellar. It will be ready to drink in September but you may keep it all winter.

Fruit Flavoured Liqueurs

Many people aren't keen on going to the effort of making wine, which can be a bit of a hit and miss affair, but fruit flavoured liquors are easy to make and always successful. At worst, they are going to be as good as the spirit you start off with.

Ratafia, Kirsch and Maraschino are all cherry based liquors, although the best known is undoubtedly cherry brandy. Brandy is the classic spirit to go with cherries, apricots, raspberries and blackcurrants. Vodka is tasteless so goes with anything, but possibly the most popular is gin which traditionally is used to make sloe gin.

Sloe Gin

Although this recipe works equally well with damsons

The bark of the blackthorn, the tree that produces sloe berries was used in medieval times to make a kind of ink. Sloes were an old remedy for cow flux and mouth ulcers, and there's also the old saying. *'Many sloes – many cold toes'* – announcing a cold winter.

Pick a few pound of fresh, ripe sloes, discarding any that show signs of damage or mould. Each sloe must be pricked several times with a fork although traditionally, they should be pricked with one of their own thorns. Place the sloes in a large jar, then add 10 oz (275g) sugar to each pound of sloes. Leave for ten days then fill the jar up with gin. Seal for two – three months then strain off the liquor and bottle.

Raspberry Vodka

Put 1lb (450g) fresh raspberries in a wide necked jar. Sprinkle over 4oz (110g) sugar and press gently with a wooden spoon until the juice begins to run. Pour over 1 pint (570ml) vodka or brandy and add a few almonds. Cover or seal the top, turning or shaking the jar every day for the first week. After about a month, strain off the fruit and filter the liquid through a double muslin or coffee filter until it is clear. Store in a cool dark place in a corked bottle.

Vodka Liqueur

Don't be put off by this huge list of ingredients, adapt them according to what you can obtain.

In a large, wide-necked jar put – 2 sticks cinnamon, 6 cardamom pods, 1 vanilla pod, 4 juniper berries, pinch of saffron, 4 roasted coffee beans, pinch of china tea, 4 cloves, 2 sprigs rosemary, 2 bay leaves, 3 sage leaves, 2 sprigs thyme, 3 lemon or orange leaves, 1 tablespoon dried lime flowers, 1 tablespoon dried lemon verbena, peel of 1 lime, 1 whole clementine or small orange (scrubbed). Pour over 570ml (1 pint) vodka. Keep peel and fruit submerged and leave to infuse for a month. Strain and add sugar syrup made from 12oz (350g) sugar and ¾ pint (425ml) water. Leave for another month then filter through muslin or coffee filter papers, bottle and cork.

far left (top and bottom): Sloes grow on the Blackthorn Bush
left: Fruit flavoured liquors like this raspberry vodka are easy to make

Honey Mead

Cave paintings in Spain from 7000BC show the earliest records of beekeeping, so exactly how long man has been using the bees wax and honey for food, medicine and cosmetic purposes is hard to say. The moorland of Derbyshire and the Peak District are thick with heather which, thanks to the bees, provides delicious heather honey. There are several varieties, the most common being ling which turns the land purple in late summer. There is also bell-heather which grows on dry rocky slopes, and a cross leaved heather which can be found on wet, boggy ground. During an average year, a hive of bees in Derbyshire can produce around 80 pounds of honey as well as pollinating many flowers, crops and fruit trees.

There are a few old superstitions related to bees, who must be told of

Jane Mosley's hand written recipe from 1690

Ar King's Way To Make Mead

Take five quarts and a pint of water and warm it, then put one quart of honey to every gallon of liquor, one lemmon, and a quarter of an ounce of motmeg (nutmeg); it must boyel til the scuem rise black, that you will have it quickly ready to drink, squeeze into it limon when you ton it. It must be cold before you ton it up

any changes in the family whether, births, marriages or deaths. They are also given a piece of any celebratory cake and the hives decorated with white wedding or black mourning ribbons. For a bee to settle on your

hand forecasts money, but if you own a hive of bees it is bad luck to exchange them for money. They can be swapped for other goods or lent, but a hive of stolen bees will never survive.

As well as spreading honey on breakfast toast or tea-time bread, from the washings of the honeycombs, the Saxons made sweet, herb flavoured mead, the drink of the gods. The name apparently originated from these early days when people celebrated a wedding for a month or 'moon' by drinking mead. True or false, a honeymoon is still part and parcel of a wedding, despite the fact that the image of mead as a celebratory drink has been replaced by sparkling wine and Champagne.

Add 3lbs (1.35kg) honey to 1 gallon (4.5ltr) of boiling water. Turn off the heat and stir well. Slice or juice 1 lemon and add along with 12 cloves and 1 cup strong black tea. Cover and allow to cool, then add champagne or ale yeast according to the manufacturers instructions. Let it ferment for 18 days then siphon into bottles and seal. Allow to stand for two weeks, when it is ready to drink.

The best Derbyshire Honey is being threatened

Places to shop and local producers that sell direct

Despite the overwhelming trend of globalisation and industrialisation of food, there are still small producers in Derbyshire dedicated to the art of cultivating the best varieties of our seasonal produce – meat, fruit and vegetables that have not been genetically improved for the sake of shelf life, nor inoculated for long-distance travel.

Home produced is fresher and healthier, and by buying at convenient local outlets, you are supporting local independent businesses the way our grand-parents did. Such committed individuals are the guardians of our culinary heritage and we use them or loose them.

Try lamb grazed on Derbyshire's limestone dales. Enjoy beef from cattle grazing wild Peakland flower meadows, hens that roam free, and bees that thrive on the local wildflowers and moorland heather. Look for ice-cream, butter, cheese, cream and milk from dairy farms that manage their woodlands and streams to benefit wildlife.

Derbyshire is an unspoilt landscape of farmland, dales and moorland

with traditional villages and small market towns. Here you will find shops as individual as the people you will meet. Alongside specialist services there are places where you can purchase good food, edible gifts and treats made with respect for nature. By supporting them, you will help rural communities to thrive once again.

Here we only have a limited space to give a brief guide to some of the businesses that hold the key to Derbyshire's culinary secrets. Space means that many had to be omitted and for that we apologise, but we hope this will tempt you to not only use these, but track down your own and thus promote Derbyshire and its traditional fare.

General Markets selling fresh produce are held throughout the region. Some like Derby, Chesterfield, Alfreton, etc are held in purpose built Market Halls that are open most days. Many are outdoor open markets and have specific market days – usually Saturday morning plus one or two others.

Derby market

Use The Local Farmers Markets

Some of the markets give extra choice and variety by combining with a Farmers Market. This is an opportunity to buy food and local products direct from local farmers, producers and craftspeople. These products will have been produced, grown, raised, baked or caught within 30 miles of the market.

Farmers Markets – monthly

Ashbourne – 3rd Saturday
Bakewell – last Saturday
    Contact: Neil McGregor
    Tel: 01629 813777
Belper – 2nd Saturday
Burton Upon Trent – last Friday
Buxton – Thursday and 2nd
    Saturday
    Contact: Pavilion Gardens
    Tel: 01298 23114
Castle Donnington – 2nd Saturday
Castleton – 1st Sunday in the month
    Contact: Lindsey Carruthers
    Tel: 01433 620699
Chesterfield – 2nd Thursday
Derby – 3rd Thursday
Heanor – 3rd Saturday
Matlock – 3rd Saturday in the month
    Contact: Catherine Rawas
    Tel: 01629 57488
Ripley - 1st Saturday
Swadlincote – 3rd Saturday
Whaley Bridge – 2nd Saturday
    Contact: Economic Development
    Tel: 0845 1297777

Buy From The Derbyshire Federation Of Women's Institutes

There are WI country markets at Bakewell Town Hall every Saturday morning and at Matlock Imperial Rooms, and Hope Valley Methodist Schoolrooms every Friday morning. Amongst other favourites are three fruit marmalade, lemon curd, apricot jam, sponge cakes and apple pies. They operate a parcel scheme so you can send a batch of goodies to a friend and have it delivered. www.wimarkets.co.uk or call 0118939 4646 for more details.

Food Fare

The annual Food Fare run by Derbyshire County Council begins with a two day event at Bolsover Castle. Held in May, the Fare is a launch pad for a week-long Derbyshire Food Festival with dozens of restaurants, shops, and food producers across the county holding events to mark festival week. Free brochure available from Tourist Information Centres or www.derbyshirefoodfestival.co.uk.

Flavour Of Peak Fare

During National Parks Week, Peak District businesses get together to serve up a feast of special events. The food and farming theme entitled *Your Countryside on a Plate*, aims to highlight local fare from producers who also help the environment. Robert Rowley, co-owner of Rowley restaurant and Bar in Baslow, uses Peak District produce to create his dishes. He said *'I'm proud of the wealth of ingredients that are available in the Peak District and feature local produce on our menu when they are in their prime – including Derbyshire Spring Lamb, wild cap mushrooms, honey from surrounding heather moorlands, Chatsworth venison, and organic Derbyshire beef.'*

Savour the Flavour of the Peak District leaflet are available at tourist information centres or go to nationalparks.gov.uk/nationalparks week

The Original Farmers Market Shop, Bakewell – Stocks food and drink produced locally. There are breads, meats, cheeses and treats from farms and producers in the Peak District National Park. Open 7 days a week.
The Original Farmer's Market Shop Ltd, 3 Market Street, Bakewell DE45 1HG. Tel: 01629 815814
www.thefarmersmarketshop.co.uk

Caudwell's Mill on the River Wye produces a range of over 20 specialist flours which include – white, wholemeal, organic and non-organic, malted flake, plain, French, pizza, coarse golden brown, pastry, self-raising, wheat flours, together with barley, buckwheat, cornflour, spelt, rye, pinhead oatmeal, oat products, mixed grain and gluten free white and brown. All at keen mill shop prices available in 1.5kg (3.2lb) 3kg (6.6lb) 6kg (13.2lb) and 16kg (35.3lb) bags.

Caudwell's historic water mill is where tradition and environment matter. It is open daily for flour sales and to see four floors of fascinating machinery.

Caudwell's Mill, Rowsley, Matlock Derbyshire DE4 2 EB
Tel: 01629 734374

The Old Cheese Shop At Hartington sells amongst others – locally-made Hartington Stilton, Buxton Blue, Dovedale Blue, Derby and Derby Sage Cheeses.

Toby's Of Wirksworth – The smallest cheese shop in the country but stacked with 100 cheeses, fresh bread, home-made soups, own label chutneys, jams and pates.

Northern Tea Merchants, 193 Chatsworth Road, Chesterfield.

Tea And Coffee For The Connoisseur

They blend and pack their own tea as well as roast and grind their own coffee. Their specialist and house blends are sold across the counter and obtainable at a wide range of outlets across the region. Choose from Ceylon Orange Pekoe, Keemun, Jasmine, Russian Caravan and Gunpowder tea. To help you choose there are background notes for each leaf or you can opt for one of the house blends that are available in tea bags.

All their coffees are pure Arabian coffees which can be purchased as whole beans or ground to order. There are many choices – Kenya Peaberry, Mocha Dijimmah, Peru Chanchamayo and Costa Rica Re Orosi or you can choose different beans to blend your own. In the café, there are tasting bars where you can try at least 50 different teas and freshly ground coffees.

Honey

We all know that bees produce honey which is used as a sweetener and is extremely good for us, but in doing so, they also supply us with wax that makes the finest honey scented candles, plus excellent furniture polish, handcream, face cream, body lotion and much more, so track down your local supplier and prepare to be amazed at the selection of honey-related produce on sale.

In case of problems, the Derbyshire Beekeepers Association can help. It was founded in 1881 and its purpose is to promote the craft of beekeeping and provide advice. During the summer they hold open aviary meetings for anyone interested in bees or the environment. Newcomers will have the chance to experience and handle bees – spare bee suits are available.

General Secretary: Mike Cross, Harlestone, Beggarswell Wood, Ambergate, Derbyshire DE56 2HF
Tel: 01773 852772
e-mail: crosssk@btinternet.com

The Honey Pot, Markeaton Park Craft Village, Derby
Tel: 01332 203893
Promoting Derbyshire honey and selling through the Markeaton outlet plus monthly markets at Belper and Bakewell.

Daisybank Apiaries, Newtown, Longnor, Buxton
Tel: 01298 83829
Honey from beehives sited throughout the Peak District National Park, producing wildflower honey and in season, blossom and heather honeys.

T M Roper, The Beehive, 48 Rowthorne Lane, Glapwell, Chesterfield
Honey from bees that roam over Hardwick Park, the ancestral home of Bess of Hardwick. Selling through local shops and farmers markets.

Organic Shop, Sound Bites, Moreldge, Derby - stocks organic fruit beers, ginger beer, cider, perry and real ale.

Organic Heaven - 4 Theatre Yard, Chesterfield S40 1PF
Tel: 0246 224666
Tim, the proprietor, specialises in finding the unusual and welcomes vegetarian requests.

Deli Ethics
Low Pavement, Chesterfield
Tel: 01246 200050

Elliotts For Natural Choice - vegetarian restaurant, health food and coffee shop in the heart of The Shambles, the ancient butchers quarters. Pauline and Mike Elliot and staff have turned this old building into a relaxing oasis.
Visit Elliotts For Natural Choice, The Shambles, Chesterfield

Pelideli, Jubilee Buildings, Crown Square, Matlock - quality and excellent traditional fresh deli produce.

Project X, Buxton - Home made cakes and panini using the best ingredients.

The Real Food Co. Wirksworth Wholesome home made pastries, rolls, cakes and savoury delights including lemon toffee, sunflower shortbread.

Willington Green Deli - Willington, Derby
Cakes, savouries and cooked meats - local and home cooked produce.

Numerous farms supply free range and organic eggs

Many have farm shops attached visit www.peakdistrictfoods.co.uk

Riber View Farm - fresh farm produce, farm grown vegetables, home made cakes, pies, jams and pickles.
Riber View Farm, Holestone Gate Road, (off the main Chesterfield/ Matlock Road) Ashover, Chesterfield S45 OJS
Tel: 01629 581954

Traditional and Rarebreed Meat Co.
Riddings Park, Wood Lane, Kniveton Wood, Ashbourne DE6 1JF
www.traderaremeat.co.uk
Tel: 01335 300059
Stall by the side of the Green Man and Black's Head, Ashbourne

top: Only the low telephone number indicates that this advert is over 60 years old
above: Support your local butcher and enjoy the best that Derbyshire can offer

J.W.Mettrick & Son, Glossop – Specialising in meat sourced from the Peak District Farms. Award winning butchers in Glossop for over 100 years and 5 generations. Have appeared on *Ready, Steady Cook* and BBC3's *Kill It, Cook It, Eat it*; voted best butcher on Radio 4's *The Food Programme*, 'Best Local Retailer' and Derbyshire Local Food Hero 2007.

Meat at Its Peak – White Peak Farm Butchery.
Beef, Lamb and Pork from the Peak District supplied and cut to your personal requirements by Richard Hobday, High Class Butcher. Poultry, local game and organic meats a speciality. A member of the Organic Farmers and Growers
The Old Slaughterhouse, Chapel Lane, Tissington, Nr Ashbourne, Derbyshire DE6 1RA
Tel: 01335 390300

Natural Game – suppliers of locally sourced game and poultry. Wild boar, venison, goose, guinea fowl, grouse, woodcock, duck, teal, pigeon, partridge, pheasant, rabbit and hare. Beautifully presented and oven ready, offered either whole or in convenient cuts and joints, enabling you to prepare a delicious meal with the minimum of effort. Ideal for informal occasions, mid-week suppers and barbeques.
Natural Game, Foston Farm, Hay Lane, Foston, Derbyshire DE65 5JP
Tel/Fax: 01889 568045

Email: naturalgame26@aol.com
www.naturalgame.co.uk

Peak Choice Ltd – traditionally reared beef and lamb from the Peak District where for generations, small family farmers have reared high quality beef and lamb. It is their traditional farming methods, together with the climate that has helped shape the wonderful landscape that millions of people enjoy today. Grazing the hills helps maintain the bio-diversity of the area which is rich in flora and fauna.

In 2005 His Royal Highness the Prince of Wales visited the Peak District and met a number of small family farmers. His conversation with them inspired the creation of this co-operative of livestock farmers to sell their high quality beef and lamb direct to consumers. The Peak District co-operative of eleven farmers now offers the very best quality lamb and beef that is born and reared in Derbyshire. It will be some of the most succulent, tender and flavoursome meat you have ever tasted because all animals graze on the lush pastures of the Peak District, all farms use only traditional farming methods to breed and rear their animals, and work to the highest standards of animal welfare.

Delivered fresh to your door, it gives you the opportunity not only to taste the regions finest produce, but to help preserve the landscape, and the livelihood of its farmers for years to come.

Peak Choice Ltd, Beeley Hill Top Farm, Hill Top, Beeley, Matlock, Derbyshire DE4 2NW
Tel: 01629 735303
www.peakchoice.co.uk

Unthank Hall Traditional Meats Holmsfield
Specialising in home reared, free range pork beef, chicken and lamb.

Peak Buffalo at Farmhouse Pantry
It was with some trepidation that the Gill family turned their back on traditional cattle farming and invested in a few water buffalo. That was back in 2000 and since then the herd has grown to 350 and the business is growing just as rapidly. At the family farm on the edge of the Peak District, where the herd graze on organic grassland, the average water buffalo will live for up to twenty years.

Many people are curious about the taste of buffalo which is very similar to beef. It has a slightly richer, fuller flavour and contains only half of the intramuscular marbling of normal beef, meaning that it contains half the fat, half the cholesterol, but twice the protein and calcium. Apart from its nutritional benefits, the production methods also help to really bring out the flavour. All buffalo meat is hung for three weeks and butchered with great attention to detail at their own farm shop, the Farmhouse Pantry at Dronfield Woodhouse. Here they sell a variety of buffalo cheese and milk which have the same health attributes and make it beneficial to allergy sufferers, lactose intolerants, etc.

The Farmhouse Pantry is a specialist butchery and delicatessen, dedicated to providing locally reared, traceable, free range and well hung meats, rare breeds and game, specialist cheeses, award winning dry cured bacon and black pudding, freezer and BBQ packs, hampers, etc, plus top class customer service and value for money.

Farmhouse Pantry sell Peak Buffalo produce at around fourteen Farmers Markets in the local area every month including Bakewell, Buxton, Castleton, Derby, Belper, Mansfield and Chesterfield, plus many summer shows and food fairs.

To find out more about this fascinating, exclusive product, or to place an order, call in at Farmhouse Pantry, 1, Barnes Lane, Dronfield Woodhouse, Derbyshire S18 8YE Tel: 01246 298123 Contact: Richard Gill on 07890 433674 or email: enquiries@farmhousepantry.co.uk

Renishaw Hall Vineyard
Renishaw Hall has been the home of the Sitwells for nearly 400 years. Sir Reresby died in the 2009 leaving his wife Penelopoe and a daughter, so the future is uncertain. This magnificent Hall and 300 acre park has been dubbed 'the best kept secret in Derbyshire', but what many people do not know is that Renishaw Hall produces its very own wine from the vineyard on the estate. When planted in 1972 in the Top Paddock of Renishaw Hall, at 53 degrees 18 minutes North, it was the most northerly vineyard in the world, as attested by the Guinness Book of Records. It held this rare

distinction for ten years until other growers followed the pioneering example.

It takes at least five years for a vine to fruit satisfactorily for wine production, but now the vineyard produces six tonnes of grapes each year. As a rule of thumb, one ton of grapes will make about 950 bottles of wine which amounts to about 2,500 bottles. The Renishaw Hall 2004 wine won a Bronze medal at the Mercian Vineyards Association wine competition, and alongside this fine wine, also available is the 'sparkling wine' perfect for that special occasion. The wine is available from the Hall and selected outlets.

Renishaw Hall is a private house and only open to the public by prior appointment but the magnificent gardens, the Gallery Café, the Stable Block Museums and Galleries are open March to September. Renishaw also hosts a wide number of special events including a Food and Farming Fair, and Vineyard Tours.

For more information contact The Events Office, Renishaw Hall, Renishaw.
Tel: 01246 432310
Fax: 01246 430760
Email: info2@renishaw-hall.co.uk
www.renishaw-hall.co.uk

Renishaw Hall Vineyard planted in 1972 was the most northerly vineyard in the world for ten years

Peak Ales

Back in January 2003 it took a leap of imagination to visualise an overgrown site with a derelict barn as a microbrewery, but virtually two years later, Cunnery Barn on the Baslow to Chesterfield road had become just that, the home of Peak Ales, traditional craft ales brewed on the Chatsworth estate. The initial recipes were well received, followed by a stronger beer, a Christmas special called *'Noggin Filler'*. The production of bottled beers was next with names like *Bakewell Best*, *DPA* and *Swift Nick* named after a notorious local highwayman.

Peak Ales are available through local sales outlets, Derbyshire pubs and through the Direct Delivery Scheme run by SIBA (The Society for Independent Brewers).
For more information contact Peak Ales, The Barn Brewery, Chatsworth, Bakewell, Derbyshire DE45 1EX.
Tel: 01246 583737
Email: info@peakales.co.uk
www.peakales.co.uk

Most Derbyshire microbreweries supply direct to specialist shops and pubs so look out for them. If you have any problems contact Derby CAMRA – www.derbycamra.org.uk. Branch Secretary – Rob Davison
Tel: 07966 200135
thelagernaut@hotmail.co.uk

The Herb Garden

First opened in 1983 by the present owners Lynne and Steve Raynor, The Herb Garden at Hardstoft has now become one of the foremost herb gardens in the country. It contains a mixture of culinary, curative and scented plants, with the Physic garden containing many rare and unusual medicinal plants from all over the world. A selection of over 300 varieties of herbs are available for sale.

For more information contact The Herb Garden, Hall View Cottage, Chesterfield Road, Hardstoft, Pilsley, Chesterfield S45 8AH
Tel: 01246 854268
www.theherbgarden.co.uk
Opening times March to September

Riverside Herb Centre

Castleton Road Hathersage S32 1EG
Tel: 01433 651055

Fresh Basil

23 Strutt Street, Belper
A gastronomic oasis well stocked with meats, cheeses and deli delights
Tel: 01773 828882
www.freshbasil.co.uk

Chatsworth Estate Farm Shop

Situated at Pilsley, 1½ miles from Chatsworth House at what used to be the stud farm and later became a milking parlour. In 1977, the Dowager Duchess of Devonshire opened the Farm Shop in the former Tack Room, selling beef and lamb from the estate. The shop has since expanded selling many other products. Open daily.
Tel: 01246 583392

Cowhouse Dairy on the Chatsworth estate now sell their ice cream to Tesco supermarkets across the region. The ice-cream, called *Udder Stuff* is produced using milk from the award wining Shottle Holstein herd to create a distinctive, rich, creamy flavour. Tesco say they are proud to support local producers and sell locally manufactured products.

Bradwell's was established 1899 and produces luxury ice-cream from the heart of the Peak District. In June 2008, they launched their new Platignum collection that have the same intensely buttery taste and quality synonymous with Bradwells but in a range of sophisticated grown up flavours
Tel: 01433 620536
www.bradwells.com

Frederick's Real Ice Cream is still providing the original 1898 recipe. Consistent winners and five times Gold Medal Winner of the Best Ice Cream in Britain award. Their fleet of familiar vans can be seen around the area and there are plans to show off the rest of their impressive fleet of vintage vehicles when they open a national ice cream transport museum in Chesterfield. Ranging from horse drawn carts, barrows, stop-me-and-buy-one tricycles, a rare 1949 Austin, and vans from every decade since, many are used in period films and nostalgic advertising. The photograph on page 71 shows their 1953 Morris Commercial (P.V.) fully restored in 2003 as seen at Chatsworth Game Fair.

Frederick's Real Ice Cream, Britannia Villa, 88 Old Hall Road, Brampton, Chesterfield
Tel: 01246 275293

Jaquest Food Specialists – deli with award winning smokehouse and retail factory shop, specialising in smoked and cured fish and meats, dry hams and cheeses – special home made chorizos, biltong and terrines. Has won 35 awards for taste and quality in national competitions.
Unit R Bolsover Business Park off Woodhouse Lane, Bolsover

Derbyshire Smokery – fish, meat and garlic smokers.
Tel: 01298 83595

Derbyshire Mushrooms – Take advantage of Derbyshire Mushrooms many years of experience and you will be able to buy strange and mysterious mushrooms, like these in the far right photograph, with total confidence. They will tell you the best way to cook them and what to

At a Farmer's market, you will find some very interesting stalls selling the more unusual produce of Derbyshire. Can you guess what this photograph below is?

serve them with. There is the Breakfast Portabello which goes with your bacon and eggs (60p per 100g). Wild Winter Charnterelle perfect with chicken (£1.80 per 100g), or the Shitake which gives a sweet woody taste when sliced and fried or added to casseroles (95p for 100g). There's the much sought after Pied De Mouton which when sliced and fried is perfect with meat, fish or added to pancakes, or the Oyster which is sweet and delicate when pan-fried in butter (£1 for 100g). The Erin G1, thinly sliced and gently sautéed in butter has a taste of porcini (£1.80 for 100g), or there's the Wild Girolle or why not try the Gourmet mixture to slice and fry in butter with shallots and herbs (£2.30 for 100g).

For a fungi feast without the guesswork, contact Derbyshire Mushrooms.
Tel: 01335 370693

Scaddows Farm Shop and Café, Ticknall

Home grown, local and conscientiously farmed fruit and vegetables from South Derbyshire growers, plus their own pick your own produce which includes strawberries, raspberries, black-berries and gooseberries plus home grown savoy cabbages and asparagus.

Pick Your Own Produce

– at Promised Land Fruit Farm above Darley Dale. See local press or telephone to find out what is in season and available.

Scotts Garden

10 Lumsdale Road Matlock
A huge allotment that grew to be 3 acres, soon 4 acres, of fully certified organic land with 200 apple, plum, damson, pear, quince and cherry trees. Sold through Matlock and Bakewell markets

Glossary of Cooking Terms and Ingredients

This list has been limited to those ingredients you might come across in old recipes, but because of the sheer volume, most aromatic and culinary roots, plants and herbs have been excluded

Alexander - horse parsley - an umbelliferous plant used for salads with stalks tasting like celery

Annise - anise, an umbelliferous plant, formerly confused with dill, the source of aniseed

Agua vita - originally unrectified alcohol; any form of spirits taken as a drink - probably brandy

Barley - a grain used for making beer and whiskey; for soups, puddings etc

Pearl barley - barley ground into small, round grains used in cooking especially soups and stews

Barley wine - an exceptionally strong beer

Biscakes - biscuits

Bores grease - lard

Boyle - boil

Brimiton - brimstone, sulphur

Burdock - a course weedy plant with leaves like the dock - bearing burrs - as in dandelion and burdock

Cardus water - juice or infusion of cardus benedictus, the Holy thistle

Cawdle - caudle - a warm drink or a thin gruel mixed with ale or wine, sweetened and spiced

Chafing dish - a portable grate or a utensil to hold burning fuel

Chalderon - chaldron or chawdron - entrails

Chewit - a dish of various kinds of meat and fish minced and seasoned. Sweet and savoury were often served together in one dish like the mincepies

Chine - backbone and adjoining flesh

Cimbals - spongy cakes or doughnut

Coffin - a pie dish or a pastry case shaped like a bread tin with 2 inch thick pastry that wasn't intended to be eaten

Coney - rabbit

Curd - a coagulated substance made from milk by the action of acids

Currans - currants

Florentine - a kind of pie or tart, especially a meat pie

Flower - flour

Fundament - buttocks and anus

Gallipot - a small, earthenware glazed pot

Groovers shreds - shavings or shreds of lead. Groover was a Derbyshire term for miner, especially the lead miner. Although this is an ingredient in old recipes, it must never be used

Hartshorn - shaved or burnt horn of harts, an early form and the chief source of ammonia

Jumbals - jumbles - a type of soft biscuit

Juyce - juice

Kickshaw - a fancy dish, dainty but insubstantial

Mallard - a wild male duck

Manchet - the finest kind of wheaten bread; a roll or small loaf

Marmalet - marmalade

Minst - minced

Motmeg - nutmeg

Neat – an animal of the ox kind, an ox, bullock, cow or heifer

Onyon – onion

Orengado – the outer yellow rind of an orange

Pennyweight – a small English unit of measure, weighing 20 to the ounce

Pill – peel

Pipkin – small earthenware or metal pot or pan

Pippin – numerous varieties of apple

Ponado – panado – a dish made by boiling bread in water to a pulp and flavouring it

Porringer – a small basin from which soup, porridge or children's food was eaten

Posit – posset – a drink made from warm milk curdled with ale, wine or other liquor, often with sugar and spice

Posnet – a small metal pot with three feet and a handle, used for boiling

Pottage – a dish of vegetables, or vegetables and meat boiled with water until soft; or a thick soup.

Purttenance – the edible inward parts of an animal

Pye – pie

Raisons of the Sunne – raisins

Rine – rind

Rocket – an annual plant used for salads

Rowle – roll

Sack – a white wine formerly imported from Spain and the canary Islands

Sallet – salad

Sal gemme – rock salt

Sawce – sauce

Sawceges – sasings – sausages

Searce – sieve through a bristle sieve

Shog – shake

Sippet – a small piece of toasted or fried bread usually served in a soup or with meat, used for dipping into gravy

Skum – skim

Smallage – wild celery or plants of the celery or parsley family especially water parsley

Spatler – spatula

Spigot or forcet – a tap on a barrel

Spinnage – spinach

Sporragus – asparagus

Stamp – pound

Stillatory – a still

Stockfish – cod and fish of the same family cured without salt, split open and dried hard in the air

Trencher – a flat piece of wood of which meat was served and carved – a large plate

Trug – a wooden milk pan, or shallow oblong basket made of wood strips

Umbles – the edible innards of an animal usually a deer

Verjuice – acid juice of green or unripe grapes, crab-apples or other sour fruits, expressed and formed into a liquor

Waa – water

The author's grandmother, Ellen (right), whose recipe collection this book is based on

Index